C ... a
f ... e works ... or
t ... NHS and for Oxford Cognitive Therapy Centre. Through ten years of clinical research with the University of Oxford, she helped to develop and evaluate cognitive behavioural treatments for social phobia and for generalized anxiety disorder. She has a special clinical interest in the use of CBT during recovery from traumatic experiences in childhood and runs training workshops on a wide variety of topics relevant to practitioners of CBT, in the UK and other countries. She is particularly interested in making the products of research available to the general public and, in addition to being the author of *Overcoming Social Anxiety and Shyness*, she is co-author of *Manage Your Mind: The Mental Fitness Guide* and of *Psychology: A Very Short Introduction*.

The *Overcoming* series was initiated by PETER COOPER, Professor of Psychology at the University of Reading and Honorary NHS Consultant Clinical Psychologist. His original book on bulimia nervosa and binge-eating founded the series in 1993 and continues to help many thousands of people in the USA, the UK and Europe. The aim of the series is to help people with a wide range of common problems and disorders to take control of their own recovery programme using the latest techniques of cognitive behavioural therapy. Each book, with its specially tailored programme, is devised by a practising clinician. Many books in the *Overcoming* series are now recommended by the UK Department of Health under the Books on Prescription scheme.

OVERCOMING
SOCIAL ANXIETY
AND SHYNESS
SELF-HELP COURSE

A 3-part programme based on
Cognitive Behavioural Techniques

Part Two: Overcoming Social Anxiety

Gillian Butler

ROBINSON
London

Constable & Robinson Ltd
3 The Lanchesters
162 Fulham Palace Road
London W6 9ER
www.overcoming.co.uk

First published in the UK by Robinson,
an imprint of Constable & Robinson Ltd 2007

Important Note

This book is not intended as a substitute for medical advice or treatment.
Any person with a condition requiring medical attention should consult
a qualified medical practitioner or suitable therapist.

ISBN: 978-1-84529-443-4 (Pack ISBN)

ISBN: 978-1-84529-571-4 (Part One)

ISBN: 978-1-84529-572-1 (Part Two)

ISBN: 978-1-84529-573-8 (Part Three)

Printed and bound in the EU

1 3 5 7 9 10 8 6 4 2

Contents

Note to Practitioners

This self-help course is suitable for a wide range of reading abilities and its step-by-step format makes it ideal for working through alone or with help from a friend or professional. The course is divided into three workbooks, and each contains a full supply of worksheets and charts to be filled in on the page – so there is no need for photocopying. If you do decide to photocopy this material you will need to seek the permission of the publishers to avoid a breach of copyright law.

Introduction: How to Use this Workbook

This is a self-help course for dealing with social anxiety and shyness. It has two aims:

1 To help you develop a better understanding of the problem

2 To teach you the practical skills you will need in order to change.

How the course works

The *Overcoming Social Anxiety and Shyness Self-Help Course* will help you understand how social anxiety and shyness develop and what keeps them going, and then to make changes in your life so that you begin to feel more confident.

These workbooks are designed to help you work, either by yourself or with your healthcare practitioner, to overcome social anxiety and shyness. With plenty of questionnaires, charts, worksheets and practical exercises, the three parts together make up a structured course.

It is important to be realistic: doing these tasks is time-consuming and sometimes difficult; it can also be rather repetitive. The key point to remember is that the exercises and worksheets are ways of working that research has shown to be helpful for many people. You could adapt the exercises to suit yourself, or change them from time to time if that makes the tasks more interesting.

Part One explains:

- What social anxiety is

- What are its symptoms and effects

- The different kinds of social anxiety and how common it is

- What shyness is and how it links with social anxiety

- How the way you think plays a major role in social anxiety

- What causes social anxiety

- What happens when you are socially anxious – and pinpointing what needs to change.

This part, **Part Two** explains:

- Some general ideas about overcoming social anxiety

- How to reduce self-consciousness

- How to change thinking patterns

- How to change the way you behave.

Part Three explains:

- How to build up confidence

- How to deal with underlying beliefs and assumptions

- How to put what you've learnt into action and overcome any practical problems

- How to become more assertive

- How to overcome bullying in your past

- How to develop relaxation skills.

How long will the course take?

Each workbook will take at least two or three weeks to work through – but do not worry if you feel that you need to give each one extra time. Some things can be understood and changed quite quickly, but others take longer. You will know when you are ready to move on to the next workbook. Completing the entire course could take two or three months, but it could take less and it could take a lot more. This will depend on the level of your social anxiety, on how quickly you are able to work and how ready you feel to make changes in your life. Take your time, and go at the pace that suits you best. You are the best judge of what you can do at any one time. If you get stuck and need a break from the work, make sure you plan when to start again.

Getting the most from the course

Here are some tips to help you get the most from the workbooks:

- These workbooks are not precious objects to be kept on the shelf – they are practical tools. So feel free not only to write on the worksheets and charts, but also to underline and highlight things, and to write comments and questions in the margins. By the time you have finished with a workbook it should look well and truly used.

- You will also find lots of space in the main text. This is for you to write down your thoughts and ideas, and your responses to the questions.

- Keep an open mind and be willing to experiment with new ideas and skills. These workbooks will sometimes ask you to think about painful issues. However, if social anxiety is distressing you and restricting your life it really is worth making the effort to do this as it will help you to overcome it. The rewards will be substantial.

- Be prepared to invest time in doing the practical exercises – set aside 20 to 30 minutes each day if you can.

- Try to answer all the questions and do the exercises, even if you have to come back to some of them later. There may be times when you get stuck and can't think how to take things forward. If this happens don't get angry with yourself or give up. Just put the workbook aside and come back to it later when you are feeling more relaxed.

- You may find it helpful to work through the workbooks with a friend. Two heads are often better than one. And if your friend also suffers from social anxiety you may be able to encourage each other to persist, even when one of you is finding it hard.

- Use the Thoughts and Reflections section at the back of the workbook to write down anything that has been particularly helpful to you. This can be anything you read (here or elsewhere), or think, or do, or anything that someone else says to you. These pages are to help you collect together your own list of helpful ideas.

- Re-read the workbook. You may get more out of it once you've had a chance to think about some of the ideas and put them into practice for a little while.

- Each workbook builds on what has already been covered. So what you learn when working with one will help you when you come to the next. It's quite possible simply to dip into different ones as you please, but you will get most out of this series of three workbooks if you follow them through systematically, step by step.

A note of caution

These workbooks will not help everyone who has problems with social anxiety and shyness. Everyone finds it hard to turn and face a problem that troubles them and doing so can make you feel worse at first. However, a few people find that focusing on social anxiety persistently makes them feel worse instead of better. This might be because they have another problem as well. The most common problems that go with social anxiety are depression and dependence on alcohol (or non-prescribed drugs). The recognized signs of clinical depression are listed below. They include:

- Constantly feeling sad, down, depressed or empty
- General lack of interest in what's going on around you
- A big increase or decrease in your appetite and weight
- A marked change in your sleep patterns
- Noticeable speeding up or slowing down in your movements and how you go about things
- Fatigue, and feeling low in energy
- An intense sense of guilt or worthlessness
- Difficulty concentrating and making decisions
- A desire to hurt yourself or a feeling that you might be better off dead

If you have become depressed because of your social anxiety, and the depression is getting in the way of using this workbook, then it would be sensible to deal with the depression first. However, many people who feel a bit depressed from time to time find that the constructive work on solving their underlying social anxiety problem also makes them feel less unhappy.

If you have had five or more of the symptoms listed above (including low mood or loss of interest) for two weeks or more, you should seek professional help from a doctor, counsellor or psychotherapist. There is nothing shameful about seeking this sort of professional help – any more than there is anything shameful about taking your car to a garage if it is not working as it should, or going to see a lawyer if you have legal problems. It simply means taking your journey towards self-knowledge and self-acceptance with the help of a friendly guide, rather than striking out alone.

SECTION 1: Starting Points

This section will help you to understand:

- The four main methods of breaking vicious cycles
- How to work out what you want to change in your behaviour
- How to keep track of your progress
- How to pace yourself
- Helpful and unhelpful ways of coping with the problem
- How to plan stress-free activities
- Useful ideas to keep in mind.

Four main methods of breaking vicious cycles

In Part One, pages 88 to 94 we looked at how vicious cycles play a major role in keeping social anxiety going. Overcoming social anxiety involves learning how to break these cycles. There are four main methods that we'll look at in turn:

1 Reducing self-consciousness

This helps you to forget yourself, so that you can behave more naturally and spontaneously when with other people. The main strategies involve consciously focusing on people and things outside yourself, and keeping more in touch with what is happening around you. You will learn how to do this in Section 2.

2 Changing thinking patterns

As we've seen in Part One, the way you think has a big effect on your social anxiety. When we are socially anxious we focus on what we think other people think about us. It therefore helps to learn how to recognize and to re-examine your patterns of thinking. Changing thinking patterns is explained in Section 3.

3 Doing things differently

Safety behaviours and avoiding things (which we looked at in Part One, pages 91 to

94) make the problem worse not better. And trying to protect yourself only makes you dread social interactions more. The answer is to face difficulties instead of avoiding them, and to take the risk of doing so without using safety behaviours for protection. You will learn how to do things differently in Section 4.

4 Building up confidence

Confidence may grow quickly or more slowly. There are some general guidelines for increasing your confidence in Part Three, Section 1. When confidence is slow to change, this may be because you also need to work on your underlying beliefs and assumptions. Section 2 in Part Three will help you identify your old negative beliefs and develop new, more positive ones. Socially anxious people tend to assume that their interactions with others will be painfully revealing. You think that others will notice your weaknesses or awkwardness; that you will be dismissed, ignored, criticized or rejected for not behaving more acceptably.

Don't aim for perfection: there's no one right way

Many people who do things 'wrong' socially are not at all anxious about it. They may:

- be awkward and abrupt

- interrupt

- get muddled or not listen to what others have to say

- tell terrible jokes or boring stories

- fall into long silences.

Despite this people want them around and make friends with them and choose them for their partners.

Not everything stands or falls according to how you behave socially.

> ### It's worth remembering...
>
> **What you do may be far less important than it seems. Being yourself is far more important.**

Feeling anxious certainly makes it hard to relax and to be yourself. And that's the case whether you are naturally interesting, charming, tedious or repetitive.

There are four things that get in the way of being yourself socially:

- Self-consciousness

- Socially anxious patterns of thinking

- Safety behaviours

- Lack of confidence.

These are the things that need to change. This workbook will show you how.

Defining your aims

Before you start, stop and think about what you want to change. You need to know what the problem is in order to start working on it, and no two people are exactly the same. The questions below are designed to help you focus on the precise aspects of your social anxiety you want to work on. It may help to refer back to Part One, Section 2 where we first looked at the effects of social anxiety on thinking, behaviour, your feelings and the signs and symptoms of your anxiety.

1 How does social anxiety affect your thinking?

For example, do you make a habit of blaming yourself if something does not go 'right'? Do you tend to remember the bad things that have happened to you, and that people have said about you? Do you forget about the good things, and the signs of appreciation and compliments you receive? Do you have trouble concentrating, or dwell excessively on past events?

_____

_____

_____

_____

_____

2 How does social anxiety affect your behaviour?

For example, do you avoid taking the lead in social situations? Do you avoid eye contact or speak quietly? Do you do things to keep yourself safe?

_____

_____

_____

_____

_____

3 How does social anxiety affect you physically?

For example, do you blush, sweat excessively or tremble?

_____

_____

_____

_____

_____

4 Which of the 'signs and symptoms' of your social anxiety bother you the most?

For example, is being tongue-tied your biggest problem or are you more concerned about blushing?

_____

_____

_____

_____

_____

5 How does social anxiety affect you emotionally?

For example, does it make you sad and depressed, anxious, angry? All of these? Or do you have other feelings, like feeling frustrated with yourself, or envious of others?

_____

_____

_____

_____

_____

_____

Remember that it is unusual for someone to have no symptoms in one of the four categories of thinking, behaviour, physical effects or emotional effects (See Part One, page 11).

If one of them is missing from your list, think again about what happens to you when you are anxious. You may, of course, be the exception to the rule. But it may also be that some of the things that happen to you have become so familiar that you no longer notice them.

Defining your goals

Now look at your answers and decide what you want to change. Be careful at this point, because it is easy to be unrealistic.

Nearly everyone sometimes feels shy or nervous, sometimes for no obvious reason and sometimes understandably. For example, you may feel anxious:

- Before making an important announcement

- When talking to someone extremely attractive for the first time

- When raising a delicate issue with someone in a position of authority

- When you have to make a complaint.

Some degree of social anxiety is perfectly normal. At times everyone has to deal with situations that are embarrassing or humiliating, or in which they are criticized, or judged, or evaluated less well than they would wish. Nothing you can do will stop such things happening.

A useful general goal might be: **I will accept these events as inevitable, but I won't let them undermine my confidence**.

If you reach this goal your social anxiety will be most likely to keep within normal levels.

More precise goals

The only problem with this goal is that it does not tell you exactly what you should try to change. If you can be more precise than this you will find it useful later on. Precise goals help you to define exactly what you want to change – for instance:

- Being able to look someone in the eye during a conversation

- No longer avoiding meeting new people because you feel fearful and vulnerable

- Being able to invite someone for a meal or to see a film.

Precise goals work best for two reasons:

1   They provide you with specific suggestions about what to work on.

2   They help you define when you have reached your goal. That way they also give you a measure of how well you are doing.

In the space below write down, as precisely as you can, what you want to change.

It may help to look back over your list of the signs and symptoms of anxiety and ask yourself what you would like to be different. What would you be able to do if you were anxious just in the way that everyone is?

Don't make your goals too demanding. Doing things in new ways, and doing new things, may well make you nervous at first. Your goals can become more ambitious as you build confidence.

My goals:

_____

_____

_____

_____

_____

Keeping track of your progress

Use the extra forms, diary pages and Thoughts and Reflections section at the end of this workbook to keep a record of your progress and keep your workbook in a safe but easily accessible place. When working on a problem like this on your own, or without help from a psychologist or counsellor or other professional, it is easy to lose track of how you are doing. Without the habit of writing, and without a safe place to keep what you have written, you will find it hard to remember important things such as how bad you were to begin with (your signs and symptoms now), what you want to change (your precise goals), and when things went right for you as well as when they went wrong.

Many people get discouraged at first because they see no sign of change. This happens for two reasons:

1 The first changes are often small

2 Small changes are easily forgotten.

When you look back over your progress in dealing with social anxiety you may tend to remember the things that went badly and forget about the things that went well. This is especially the case if these just seem to be 'normal' activities for others, like answering the doorbell, or chatting to a neighbour, or walking across a room when you know everyone can see you.

One way to deal with this problem is to keep using and referring to this workbook to monitor your progress. Write down what you do differently every day before you can forget, and your plans about what to do next. Look at how you did the exercises at first and how you improved later on. That way you'll get a real sense of achievement.

Trying things out and pacing yourself

Trying new things is an essential part of dealing with your problem. Overcoming social anxiety helps your confidence to grow, and deciding to do something about the problem can give you a real boost.

Some of the things you try out may also be surprisingly enjoyable, but at the same time doing this work takes courage. The best strategy is to give yourself regular assignments, rather like doing homework, and to accept that you will have to take some risks – when you feel ready to do so.

Doing things in a new way helps to break the old patterns. It can feel dangerous at first – like learning to swim or to drive on the motorway in pouring rain and bad light. You will not have to do anything you consider too difficult – or anything really threatening or risky. You should also plan your homework tasks so that you can progress at your own pace. There is no rule about how fast you should go, as everyone is different.

Other people can make suggestions about what you might do, but only you can try them out. So you will need to find time for this work. If you are a very busy person you may have to decide when to give a high priority to working on your social anxiety, and decide what to give up in order to make time for it.

Just as when you learn anything new, like a new language for instance, you will improve faster if you work at it regularly. Leaving large gaps when you forget about it altogether is likely to mean that you lose headway. The gains you make may be lost again as they never had a chance to be put on a sure foundation.

Helpful and unhelpful ways of coping with the problem

Everyone who has a problem with social anxiety tries to deal with it in their own way. Many ideas about how to cope can be imaginative, helpful and productive. Your own strategies may be of this kind, and you may want to keep on using them. If so, you should test them against the following principle:

Helpful strategies are those that have no long-term disadvantages.

Helpful strategies

Sections 2, 3 and 4 of this workbook and Sections 1 and 2 of Part Three explain in detail the strategies that researchers have found to be very helpful. Other helpful strategies include:

- Developing your skills, talents or hobbies, whether on your own or with other people

- Learning how to relax (which is described briefly in Part Three, Section 6)

- Finding ways of expressing yourself and your feelings about social anxiety including talking to someone, writing about what you feel, speaking about it into a dictaphone or tape recorder, drawing pictures of how it feels, and expressing your feelings through music, or dance, or physical exercise. We looked at this strategy in Part One, page 41. It can help you physically as well as psychologically.

Unhelpful strategies

Less helpful ways of coping with social anxiety tend to have beneficial effects in the short term, or immediately you do them, but to have harmful effects in the long term.

Seeking reassurance

It often helps to hear someone say reassuring things such as:

- 'Don't worry.'
- 'There's nothing seriously wrong with you.'
- 'It will probably get better in the end.'
- 'It's always nice to see you.'

But reassurance does not last. It calms you down temporarily without solving any problems. It is rather like 'getting a fix': the better it works, the more you want to seek it out next time you feel bad. Taking charge of finding your own, lasting solutions to the problem will be far more helpful in the long run.

Do you seek reassurance as a way of coping with social anxiety? Describe what you do and the effect it has here.

_____

_____

_____

_____

_____

_____

Using alcohol

Using alcohol to make you feel less anxious is another common, but unhelpful, way of coping. It is easy to understand why it is tempting. Alcohol plays a part in many different kinds of social situations, and it does often have an immediate calming effect. It makes people feel less shy and it can make them more talkative.

But there are many dangers associated with using alcohol to solve social problems.

- You may become addicted to alcohol and not be able to cope without it.

- You may drink too much and lose control of your behaviour.

- You're likely to suffer health effects including dehydration, headaches and nausea.

- You may also suffer long-term health effects if you use alcohol too frequently and in large quantities, including weight gain and liver damage.

You may not be aware that alcohol also has a depressant effect. After the initial effect of dampening down your feelings of anxiety it is more likely to make you feel worse than better, and it interferes with sleep patterns. Many people think that they will sleep better if they have a drink or two, and indeed they do often fall asleep more quickly after drinking than they would otherwise. But they often wake during the night and then find it hard to go back to sleep again.

Do you use alcohol as a way of coping with social anxiety? If so, use the diary on page 11 over the next two weeks to record how much you drink, when and how you feel at the time and then how you feel the next day. A sample entry has been filled in as a guide. You'll find extra forms at the back of this book.

Street drugs (recreational drugs) often have similar effects to alcohol. If you are using these to help you feel less anxious then it will also be helpful to use the diary to monitor your usage and the physical and psychological effects at the time you use them and the day after.

Planning stress-free activities: a sense of proportion

Anxiety and problems can come to dominate your life and it may become hard to think about anything else. One way of beginning to get a new perspective on the problem, and on what it means for you, is to make sure that you involve yourself in things that have nothing to do with social anxiety at all, and that you enjoy.

Here are some things that you may find helpful:

- **Physical activities** like exercise or gardening

- **Recreational activities** like listening to music, reading, exploring new places, watching TV, playing computer games

- **Learning something new** like how to plaster a wall or cook Mexican food

- **Creative activities** of all kinds: painting, drawing, writing, playing an instrument, home-making and so on

Alcohol use record

Date and event	Units of alcohol	How I felt at the time	How I felt the next day
Friday, birthday drinks for Ben at work	Three cocktails, three large glasses of wine	Nervous and shy; better after the alcohol.	Awful; headache and bad night's sleep. Tired, irritable and moody in the morning.

Whatever you enjoy, or used to enjoy, you should do more of. Whatever you are curious about, you should start to explore. Try to limit the effect social anxiety has on your life so that it does not affect other sources of pleasure and satisfaction.

Make a list here of some of the activities you enjoy now, or used to enjoy, or think you might enjoy.

Enjoyable activities:

_____

_____

_____

_____

_____

_____

The first approach to feeling isolated, or lonely

Being socially anxious can make you feel cut off from others. It can make it hard to build up a group of friends and to develop intimate relationships. The main aim of this book is to explain how to overcome this anxiety. We assume that you want to be able to become involved with others more easily and more often, that you do not want to feel isolated and lonely.

However, it is possible to recognize the value of companionship while still valuing solitary activities. It is important, and healthy, to be able to do things on your own, and to enjoy doing them.

In the space below make a list of activities you can enjoy doing by yourself. To help you do this, think about:

• Things other people you know do by themselves

• Things that you used to do by yourself at other times in your life

If you have more solitary and lonely times than you want at the moment, try to fill at least some of them with enjoyable or interesting or challenging or creative activities that you can do – and enjoy – on your own. For example, if you enjoy seeing new places, then it would be a good idea to plan an expedition. Don't let difficulties such as having to travel and to eat on your own get in the way.

Things I can do by myself:

_____

_____

_____

_____

_____

_____

Some helpful points to bear in mind

Here are some general points that may help you while you are working on your social anxiety.

- Learn to recognize the vicious cycles that keep the problem going; then you can work at breaking them. See Part One, Section 7.

- You will need time and you will need to persist if you are to make the most of the ideas in this book. Don't worry if change comes more slowly than you would wish.

- Keep the problem in perspective. This means both keeping a check on the way you are thinking, and making sure that you do not let the problem dominate your waking life. Remember to leave time in your life for those things that you enjoy, or are interested in, and are good at.

- If you are having difficulty doing things differently, then it may be helpful to start with easy things first. Work up to harder ones as your confidence grows.

Don't give up!

The more you do, the more you will improve. Sometimes things will go well, sometimes not, and so you may feel discouraged at times. You will be more likely to build your confidence if you can keep going despite these normal ups and downs. Everyone has good days and bad days, and problems always seem worse on a bad one. If you expect a few of these normal fluctuations they will be less likely to set you back when they happen.

It is important to be realistic. Doing the exercises described here takes time and can be difficult. Sometimes it may even be rather tedious, boring and repetitive, or seem unnecessary. The key point to remember is that the exercises and worksheets are examples of ways of working that other people have found useful. To make them more useful to you you could adapt them to suit yourself, or change them from time to time if that makes the tasks more interesting. But do remember to keep track of what you do.

Answers to some of the questions that people often ask

Should you work at becoming socially skilled?

The answer is 'yes, if you want to'; but remember that:

- **You can pick up these skills as you go**. Most people acquire their 'social skills' without being taught the 'rules of the game', just as they learn to ride a bicycle. You do not have to understand how it works in order to do it.

- **There is no right way of doing things**. You can be successful without being socially skilled. Many people get on well with others but are not good at these things, or find them difficult. Being socially skilled neither makes people love you nor prevents them criticizing you.

- **Skills may come naturally once you feel less anxious**. Being anxious, worried or fearful makes it hard to use your social skills.

- **Being flexible will allow you to be more spontaneous**. Let yourself adapt as the situation demands rather than constantly trying to practise your social skills or to learn precise rules of the game. This will allow your social life to flow more naturally.

There are many things that people learn to do socially. Here is a list of some of them. You could probably add some more of your own:

- Listening to what others have to say

- Talking in such a way that others listen to what you say

- Looking at others when you speak to them, and using non-verbal ways of communicating

- Making conversation – in general, or to someone important like your boss, or someone you would like to go out with

- Introducing people to each other

- Saying no when you think it would be right to do so, or sticking up for yourself

- Telling someone they have done something that makes you angry

- Being aware of and sensitive to other people's feelings

- Expressing your own feelings and opinions

- Asking someone to do something for you.

- Others (write in):

_____

_____

_____

_____

_____

_____

All of these skills develop with practice. A few other specific skills such as assertiveness and relaxation can also be useful if you are socially anxious. They are described in Part Three, Sections 4 and 6.

How can you learn about conventions?

Conventions are recognized ways of doing things, or patterns of behaviour. Many people feel uncomfortable or unconfident if they do not know the conventions, for instance if they do not know which fork to use, or what clothes to wear. Turning up in jeans when everyone else is dressed in their best (or vice versa) can be embarrassing.

This may especially be a problem for people with social anxiety because being the 'odd one out' attracts attention and so seems to encourage other people to judge or evaluate you.

There are several ways to learn about social conventions:

1 Ask

Would you mind if someone asked you about what was the right way to do something? Would it be better to admit that you do not know, or to do 'the wrong thing'? Maybe it would be more polite to ask. For example, at a formal dinner party could you say 'I'm sorry, but I'm not sure where I should sit? Or ask 'Do you know if there's a seating plan?'

Use the space below to write down some ways in which you could politely ask for more information about how to behave in a social situation. First describe the particular situation; for example, a special birthday party, a formal work dinner or a barbecue for friends. Next, write down possible questions.

The social event or situation:

_____

Questions I could ask to get more information:

_____

_____

_____

_____

_____

2 Use the information provided

Sometimes information is there but you are too confused to take it in (for example, notices about wearing ties, or not smoking, or laying out forks in the order they would be used in). Learning to relax before a social event can help you to be more observant and take in helpful information when you're there. We look at relaxation techniques in Part Three, Section 6.

3 Observe

Watch what other people do before you make a move yourself, for example before asking someone to dance. Listen to how others start a conversation, and look at the way they dress. Observe things that people take for granted, such as whether their clothes are clean and their hair washed. Look for things that tell you what is socially 'acceptable' in a particular setting, and what is not. People in different places, interacting in different ways, develop different conventions, so there is no one right way. Watch out for upsetting thoughts if you break a convention. In five years' time, who will remember that you sat in someone else's place or spoke out of turn at a meeting? That you had a moment when you became flushed and distressed, or that you could not hide the fact that you were bored or irritated? It is not a law of the land that you have to obey conventions. Indeed, that may be why they are called 'conventions' rather than rules or laws.

Questions about anxiety

Finally, before we start working through the practical exercises in Sections 2, 3 and 4, let's look at some questions people often ask about social anxiety.

Can a severe bout of anxiety do physical harm?

No. In particular, remember that increased heart rate caused by anxiety alone will not damage your heart any more than increased heart rate caused by exercise or excitement.

Can prolonged anxiety do you mental harm?

The symptoms of anxiety and panic by themselves, however severe, do not mean that you are developing a serious mental disorder or going insane. They are normal reactions developed to protect you in case of a real (rather than a social) emergency.

Does being anxious make you tired?

Yes. When you are anxious you may find it hard to cope with a normal day. Being anxious and tense is a drain on your energy. Once you have become less anxious, you will find you have more energy for other things. This is one reason why it is important that you balance the anxiety in your life with activities that you find relaxing and enjoyable. See Part Three, Section 6 for information about how to relax.

What if I am depressed as well as anxious?

Many people have periods of feeling fed up, miserable or sad if their social anxiety goes on a long time. But these feelings often lift when they start working on the problem and realize that there is something they can do about it.

Depressed feelings make it harder to keep trying, but they are not a reason for giving up. If your anxiety improves your other feelings are likely to do so as well.

However, if you feel severely depressed; and if you, or people who know you, are worried about the effects that being depressed is having on you, then you should talk to your doctor about it.

Questions about getting better

Should I give up trying for a while and take a good rest?
Not if having a rest becomes a way of not facing up to the problem or working out how to overcome it.

If I grin and bear it, will the problem go away by itself?
Possibly. Some problems of this kind do eventually diminish. But if you learn what to do to overcome the problem then you are likely to improve sooner. Also, you will be able to 'nip it in the bud' should you start to feel anxious again later.

Was I born this way, so that there is nothing I can do about it?
You may have been born more sensitive to stress than other people, or think of yourself as a shy sort of person. We looked at this in more detail in Part One, Section 6. But this does not mean that you cannot learn how to overcome social anxiety and make many changes for the better in your life.

Should I go on searching for a 'cure'?
Nobody can cure you of anxiety altogether, as it is a normal part of everyday life. However, if you learn how to think and behave differently you will come to react to social situations differently also, and will be able to cope with them much better.

Would it be helpful to take some medication?

It could be. There are many different kinds of drugs now available for treating both anxiety and depression, and new ones are coming out all the time. Some of them are extremely effective.

However, there are many issues to consider when making this decision. Although drugs may help you temporarily, they may not solve the problem in the long run, and some of them become less effective if you take them regularly, so that you need more to achieve the same effect.

Also, if you come to rely on drugs, they may undermine your confidence in handling things without them. Using them regularly as a 'prop' makes it harder to build confidence in your own ability to overcome the problem. Also the problem may come back again when you stop taking them.

So this could be a difficult decision that it would be best to discuss with your doctor. Whatever you decide, it is worth using the ideas in this book to work at overcoming the problem yourself.

If you are already taking some medication that you find helpful, then there is no need to stop taking it in order to use the ideas in this book. The two different ways of helping yourself can work together.

However, if you make two changes at once, and you feel better because of them, then it is not possible to know which one helped – or whether they both did. So it is probably better to start one new thing at a time: either using medication or using the ideas in this book.

It's worth remembering...

Learning that you can make positive changes in the ways that you think and behave will help you to build confidence in yourself. This is one of the most effective ways to reduce your social anxiety in the long run.

What if social anxiety is only a part of the problem?

It is quite common for people who have been socially anxious for a long time to have some other difficulties as well. For example:

- Some people suffer from periods of depression.

- Others have difficulty being appropriately assertive. They can be too passive and accommodating or overly hostile and aggressive.

- Many people have occasional panic attacks in particularly stressful situations.

- Many socially anxious people describe themselves as 'born worriers', and may find that at times they are beset by worries of all kinds, not just about their social lives.

Do any of these difficulties also affect you? Describe your experiences here.

_____

_____

_____

_____

_____

_____

As we discussed earlier, most people know well that they feel less anxious after having a couple of drinks, and so it is quite common for people to start using alcohol, or various other substances, to help them feel more relaxed in company. When this becomes a habit, or the only way of coping with the loneliness or isolation that can accompany social anxiety, then one problem can easily lead to another.

If you have other difficulties as well as social anxiety, this book could still be helpful. You may have to think about which problem to tackle first, or to ask someone's advice about this, but it is still worth a try. When you decide that it is the right time to start, work carefully through the book, and try not to give up even if change seems to come slowly.

It's worth remembering...

It is best to stick to one thing at a time when trying to make important changes in your life.

Summary

1   Keep using and referring to your workbook to keep track of your progress.

2   Write down your own signs and symptoms of social anxiety. Try to find at least one in each of the four categories: those that affect your thinking, your behaviour, your body and your feelings or emotions.

3   Define your aims as precisely as you can. Ask yourself: what do you want to be different?

4   Check with yourself: how will you find the time for your social anxiety work? Can you set aside a time to think about it properly once a week? And plan to do something towards realizing your aims most days?

5   Go at your own pace. No two people are the same, and it is more important to discover what works for you, and how quickly you are able to change, than to be influenced by what other people do.

SECTION 2: Reducing Self-Consciousness

This section will help you understand:

- The effects of self-consciousness

- How to reduce self-consciousness

- How to deal with feeling uncomfortable and awkward

- How to focus on what is happening around you.

Self-consciousness comes from focusing your attention inwards, on to yourself so that you become painfully aware of what is happening to you. At its worst, self-consciousness dominates your attention. It makes it difficult to think of anything else but your inner experience – and this can become totally paralysing.

A bout of self-consciousness can affect you in any social situation, regardless of how well you know the people you are with. Entering a room full of people, or saying goodbye when you leave, are situations which are especially likely to provoke it. This may be because at those times it is more difficult to do what is expected of you socially without drawing attention to yourself.

Self-consciousness goes with feeling that you stand out, that other people are looking at you, and, for socially anxious people, that goes with feeling vulnerable. It can be provoked, or made worse, by becoming aware of any of the symptoms of social anxiety. For example all these symptoms could make you feel self-conscious:

- Not being able to concentrate or think straight

- Feeling nervous

- Noticing how hot you are

- Hearing the sound of your own voice

- Having the impression that you are being scrutinized

- Doing something clumsy

- Catching a glimpse of your hand movements

- Worrying about some aspect of your appearance or your performance

- Trying to make sure that you don't say anything stupid

- Checking out how you are coming over

- Rehearsing what to say.

Losing yourself in order to find yourself

The less self-conscious you are, the easier it is to be yourself, and to join in naturally with what is going on around you. The most helpful strategy to learn in order to become less self-conscious is how to direct your attention on to other things. In this way you break the pattern of inward focusing which makes you so self-aware. If you can 'lose yourself' or 'forget yourself', you will be better able to 'find yourself' – to be your 'real self' and feel comfortable being that way.

Remember, there is nothing new or special that you have to learn in order to be able to interact more naturally with other people. Things will work out fine when you learn to become less self-conscious about it.

When you're watching a gripping film, or studying a timetable in order to decide which train to catch, concentrating on what you are doing means that you notice little else. The cinema may be draughty and the railway station crowded and noisy, but these things are irrelevant to what you are doing. They can go completely unnoticed while you're focused on what you're doing. If you gave other people, and things outside yourself, a similar degree of attention there would be less space left for noticing the discomfort and tumult inside you.

The effects of self-consciousness

Feeling self-conscious makes all kinds of symptoms worse:

- The sensations themselves

- The need for self-protection and to resort to using safety behaviours

- The inability to act naturally, and

- Many kinds of socially anxious thinking.

At the same time self-consciousness reminds you of how unpleasant the symptoms of social anxiety are and increases your fear that others will notice them. It focuses your attention on what others might think and on the fear of how they might react, and it makes you feel uncertain and unconfident.

The inner world versus the outer world

All of these reactions make it difficult to become fully involved in social situations. Instead, your mind is occupied with what happens inside you: with your concerns, thoughts and worries. There's not much brain space left over for picking up other kinds of information. What information does get through tends to be hazy, insufficient or inaccurate.

This is one reason why being self-conscious interferes with your ability to carry out ordinary activities in a natural and smooth way. You're literally not paying full attention. It's why your elbow knocks the flowers from the table, or your tie lands in the soup. Or why you hesitate when greeting someone between the handshake and the kiss, and suddenly feel that you do not know what you are expected to say or do, or where to put yourself. It is why you can't follow a conversation easily, or make sense of what the last person just said.

What research tells us

We know this is happening from research as well as from what people say about their anxiety. Researchers have found that socially anxious people remember fewer details of the situations they have been in compared with other people. They also rate other people's facial expressions more negatively than others do. It is as if they know a great deal about themselves, but rather less about things outside themselves. And they use their socially anxious imagination to fill in the gaps.

People who aren't socially anxious tend to see a situation as risky depending on factors such as what might happen or who might be there. By contrast socially anxious people tend to see a social situation as risky or not depending on how they might feel. And the worse they feel the more dangerous the situation seems to be. Their own thoughts and feelings are the basis on which they see the risks involved in the outside world.

The centre of a vicious cycle

Self-consciousness is at the centre of the vicious cycles that keep social anxiety going so it's very important to try to reduce its impact. Let's look at some real-life examples of the effect of self-consciousness.

The case studies below show how often the effects of self-consciousness do not come separately, but are mixed up together. As you read through these case studies try to notice the many different ways in which feeling self-conscious works to keep the problem going. Then answer the questions that follow each story.

CASE STUDY: James

James and his girlfriend were going to have a meal with her parents. He did not know them well yet, and as soon as they walked in at the door he thought to himself that they were sizing him up. Suddenly he became aware of every movement he made, and every-thing he thought of saying seemed to first present itself to be checked and then was immediately censored before he said it.

His mouth felt too dry to talk, and he felt too awkward to ask for a drink. All he could think about was his inner foolishness, and the need for the situation to come to end. 'How long is this going to last?' was the question in his mind.

Then suddenly everyone was laughing, and he had clearly missed the joke. He had the terrible thought that he must have done something odd, or said something stupid, and that they were laughing at him.

Later his girlfriend told him that no one had noticed anything at all. Although he had been rather quiet at first, to her this had seemed understandable – and only natural.

1 What did James think when he arrived for dinner?

_____

2 What did James notice? What was he paying attention to?

_____

_____

_____

_____

3 How did James's self-consciousness affect:

The way he behaved?

_____

_____

The way he felt?

_____

_____

4 What did James notice of what was actually happening around him?

_____

_____

_____

_____

_____

5 What did the other people present notice about his behaviour? How odd did they think it was?

_____

_____

_____

_____

_____

CASE STUDY: Sandra

As Sandra came into the office the head of her department stopped as he rushed by and asked if she would make a couple of announcements for him at their group's early morning meeting. He had unexpectedly been called out, and as he hurried away, he thrust a piece of paper into her hand with something scribbled on it.

Sandra was extremely nervous about having to do this and she knew that the longer she had to worry the worse she would feel. So she decided to do it immediately, and walked straight into the meeting room without even taking her coat off.

The meeting was just starting, so she went to the front of the room, explained why she was there and read out the first part of the message. But the second part had been scribbled so hurriedly that it was almost impossible to read. She hesitated, and suddenly she heard her voice dying away.

As the silence went on she was convinced that all eyes were upon her, standing there awkwardly, still in her overcoat. In her mind's eye she had a vision of how she must look. She described herself later as childish-looking; tall, shapeless like a lanky adolescent, with the bit of paper fluttering in her trembling hands, peering at it short-sightedly for a clue as to what it might mean.

It seemed like an eternity before she thought of explaining that she could not read his writing and passed the note to someone else. When they could do no better than she had done, her confusion died away, but only partly. The image of seeing herself as others saw her haunted her for the rest of the day. Each time it came back she was covered with confusion again, feeling hot and foolish, as if stripped of all protective armour.

1 What were the thoughts or images that went through Sandra's mind as she tried to read the message?

_____

_____

_____

_____

_____

2 What did she notice about herself?

_____

_____

_____

_____

_____

3 How much was Sandra paying attention to the meeting? How much attention was she paying to herself?

_____

_____

_____

_____

_____

CASE STUDY: Andrew

Andrew was talking on the telephone when three people he knew walked into the room, talking loudly to each other. As he became aware that they could hear everything he was saying, he lowered his voice. One of them noticed this and told the others to be quieter, and in the hush that followed his voice appeared to Andrew to echo round the room. He could no longer concentrate on what he was saying, or understand properly what was being said to him. He spoke even more quietly, until he was almost whispering, and the silence around him appeared to grow.

Frantically he wondered how to end the conversation, and so he made some excuse (that later he could not remember), and hung up. He was astonished when he looked up that the others were no longer there. They must have walked through the room and out the other side. It was the thought that they might have been listening and judging him that had made him so self-conscious. It had dominated his thoughts to the extent that he was unaware of anything else.

1 What are the effects of Andrew's self-consciousness

on his behaviour?

_____

on his feelings?

_____

on his thoughts?

_____

2 At what point did Andrew notice that the other people in the room had left?

_____

_____

_____

_____

_____

_____

Summary of the effects of self-consciousness

All three case studies show how self-consciousness can have a dramatic effect on how you behave, what you notice and how you think and feel.

1 Self-consciousness focuses attention on to yourself so you notice:

   - Sensations such as feeling hot (like Sandra), or a dry mouth (like James)

   - Behaviours, like fiddling with your hands, or in Sandra's case, trembling

   - Emotions (or feelings), like feeling embarrassed, or in James's and Sandra's case, feeling stupid or foolish

   - Thoughts, like 'They think I'm peculiar', or in James's case, 'They're laughing at me', and in Andrew's case, 'how can I end this conversation?'

2 You tend to see yourself as you suppose others see you. For example, Sandra thought everyone at the meeting saw her as 'childish-looking'.

3 It makes you want to protect yourself: by keeping yourself safe or escaping from the situation. James, for example, focused on when the dinner would end and he could get away. Andrew tried to speak as quietly as possible.

4 It is difficult to notice other things accurately at the same time. You may, however, notice some things of particular significance to you, like a fleeting expression on someone's face, without noticing much else. For example, Andrew didn't notice that the other people who had been talking had actually left the room – that was why there was silence. And he couldn't understand properly what was being said to him.

5 You feel increasingly at risk, and all the effects we've listed above grow stronger, and make the problem worse, the longer they go on. As we've seen, Andrew's level of panic grew to the point where he had to end his phone conversation.

How self-consciousness affects you

Think about some specific instances of self-consciousness from your own experience. Try to think through one or two of them in detail. Take your time.

Describe the first example here:

_____

_____

_____

_____

_____

Now describe the second example:

_____

_____

_____

_____

_____

As we saw in Andrew's story, self-consciousness makes you miss out on accurate information about what is going on. You may find this hard to believe in your own case. Obviously you won't remember any information you never picked up in the first place. And you may have filled any gaps using your own imagination. When your attention is turned inwards it becomes difficult to do the following things:

- Follow what people are saying

- Notice what they are doing

- Judge how they are really reacting.

You may imagine that other people can see all the signs of anxiety and inadequacy that you feel. And you may believe that other people are judging you negatively when they see them.

Many of the conclusions that people reach when they feel self-conscious are based on their inner experience of the feelings, sensations and actions that they find so distressing: 'I said so little, and felt so embarrassed that they could see how inadequate and useless I am.' It is as if they are so aware of these things that they suppose that other people must be so too. For each specific situation you described above, answer these two questions:

1 What conclusions about yourself did you come to when you felt self-conscious?

_____

_____

_____

_____

_____

_____

2 What conclusions do you think other people came to about you?

_____

_____

_____

_____

_____

_____

Your conclusions may be negative; they may also be very inaccurate. We will help you find new ways to behave in these situations so that you are less focused on yourself and more aware and observant of what's happening around you. When this happens you will start to feel less uncomfortable and distressed and you'll also start getting a more accurate picture of what's really going on.

Reducing self-consciousness

The key to reducing self consciousness is to learn how to focus more of your attention on what is happening outside yourself, instead of on what is happening inside. You need to forget yourself enough to become absorbed in your social life instead.

To do this, you need consciously to practise switching your attention away from yourself and on to other things. This includes the other people around you – the source of your fear. Being curious will help you do just this.

Become an observer

Your task is to watch what happens, and to think openly about it, just as a scientist might when investigating a new field. Having this attitude helps you to interact with others more smoothly and more naturally.

> ### It's worth remembering...
>
> **Listen to what people say, and look at what they do before coming to a judgement about how they are reacting to you.**

Think of yourself as exploring and investigating so as to reach a balanced opinion. Your opinion should be one that an outside observer of the same situation would also agree with; someone who is not caught up in the action. Try to make sure that you are not relying on guesswork. This is highly likely to be influenced by your expectations and assumptions.

How to do it

Of course, this is easier said than done. As you know, when you feel bad it is difficult not to think about yourself, and to turn your attention away from your distress. It is helpful to think of learning to divert your attention as a two-stage process:

1 Deciding not to think about how bad you feel

2 Focusing on what is happening around you.

Let's look at each of these in more detail.

Stage 1: Deciding not to think about how bad you feel

It would be useful for unpleasant thoughts, feelings and sensations to grab your attention if the risk involved was a real one, and you really were in some danger. But most of the time when you feel socially anxious, there really is no danger.

In Section 3 you will learn the thinking skills to help you to deal with thoughts about social danger and catastrophe.

Secondly, ask yourself whether there is anything to be gained by dwelling on how uncomfortable, embarrassed or awkward you feel.

- Does it have any benefits?

- Does it give you any advantages?

- Do you think that it might help to prepare you for the worst?

- Does thinking about how bad you feel allow you to make your escape before the thing that you fear most actually happens?

Thoughts such as these are common. But in fact, focusing your attention on yourself, or self-consciousness, has far more disadvantages than advantages.

In the space below see if you can write down the advantages for you of not thinking about how bad you are feeling. Then make the decision to turn your attention away from these thoughts when they come into your head – which undoubtedly they will, at least at first.

When your heart is thumping and you cannot find the words with which to express yourself, the **disadvantage** of paying attention to your feelings is that it makes you worse: increasingly self-aware and self-conscious. Before long you just wish that the ground would open and swallow you up.

One **advantage** of forcing yourself to focus on people and things around you is that it gives you some recovery time. Use the case studies at the start of this chapter, and the summary of the effects of self-consciousness on page 28, to help you to think of more advantages for you. Write them down here.

Advantages of not thinking about how bad you're feeling:

_____

_____

_____

_____

_____

_____

_____

Stage 2: focusing on what is happening around you

The aim of this strategy is to help you to rely less on guesswork. You should try to give more attention to the person or people with whom you are interacting, so that you can:

- Listen better to what is being said

- Look at the other people involved

- Notice their reactions as well as your own.

Don't focus 100 per cent of your attention on other people and forget yourself entirely. Instead try to achieve a balance between internal and external focusing, between your own thoughts and feelings and the outside world. You would not, for example, keep your eyes fixed (unnaturally) on someone else, but rather allow yourself to make eye contact and to look away just as you might if you did not feel anxious at all.

This might seem very difficult at first. One way to make it easier is to give yourself something to do when you're in a social situation. For example, you could:

- Observe what the other person or people are wearing and how stylish or not you think they are

- Try to guess what they might be feeling or what sort of day they've had

- Work out what their occupation might be.

Find something about the other people you're with that interests you. Imagine that you were going to describe them to someone else and make mental notes about them.

Make a list here of some of the other things you could observe or do to keep your attention focused on other people and away from yourself.

_____

_____

_____

_____

_____

_____

When your mind wanders

So you've decided not to think about how unpleasant a social experience is or how bad you are feeling, and you've turned your attention to something else. You may find, however, that your attention wanders off, or appears to be grabbed once again by your internal sensations and feelings.

This is entirely normal. Unless we are especially relaxed and sleepy, our attention constantly shifts, as if we were always scanning and examining our surroundings. So, even when you have made the 'right' decision, and have succeeded in making yourself focus on something outside yourself, you may find that you quickly lose the new focus.

When this happens, just repeat your original plan. Turn your attention outwards again. It may help to **think** about something external (and unthreatening), and to do something to help engage your attention as well. For example, you could think about how nice the other person's hair looks and ask them where they get it cut.

The two-way experiment

The two-way experiment can help you to learn how to control what you pay attention to. It involves trying things out in two completely different, contrasting ways, and comparing what you notice and what you feel on the two occasions.

You need to become curious and find out what happens if you pay attention exclusively to yourself, even exaggerating what happens when you feel self-conscious. Then you need to do the exact opposite. That means forcing yourself to pay attention exclusively to someone else or to something outside of yourself.

It takes some courage to carry out this experiment, and you need to think carefully about it before you start.

- Where and when could you do it?

- How will you explore the difference between the two occasions?

Let's take a detailed look at an example of a two-way experiment. You'll find extra copies of this sample experiment with space to write your answers to the questions at the back of this workbook.

The supermarket queue experiment

Choose a setting when you are not much involved, or even not involved at all, with the people around you. This could be standing in the supermarket queue, or sitting on a bus or train with other people nearby.

Step 1: Focus on yourself

Notice all the physical sensations that you can feel.

- Are you hot or cold?

- Are you hungry or tired?

- Do you have any aches or pains?

- Can you feel your clothes? Is anything too tight or too loose?

- What are your feelings and emotions?

- Is anything particular running through your mind? Any thoughts or images? Or impressions? Or memories?

Continue doing this for three to five minutes. If your mind wanders, then bring it back to yourself. It is all right to let your mind wander on to your own concerns and worries, if you like, but if it wanders away from yourself then just bring it back again and keep up the internal focus.

Then ask yourself the two assessment questions:

1 How did you feel?

2 What did you notice?

- Were you surprised by how many things were going on inside?

- Did you become more aware of your inner experiences?

- If so, did this change them in any way? Make them more or less intense?

- And what did you notice?

- Do you know anything about what the other people around you looked like? About their expressions, appearance, conversations and actions, for example?

- Could you describe something about one of them? Or describe exactly what one of them was doing while you were focusing on yourself?

You should make sure that your answers are clear to yourself. Make a mental note of them, or write them down on the worksheet, before going on with the experiment.

Step 2: Reverse the experiment

The next step is to reverse the experiment. For another few minutes try to focus your attention exclusively outside yourself. Notice something about each of the people around you. Without obviously staring at them, see if you can be sensitive to something about them, such as:

- How they might feel

- How lively or energetic or lethargic they seem

- How physically fit they might be.

Try to observe anything you can think of that might be of interest to you.

If it seems natural and appropriate, then talk to them. Allow yourself to get into conversation, and allow your curiosity to lead the way.

Then ask yourself the two assessment questions again:

1 What did you feel this time?

2 What did you notice this time?

Make sure your answers are clear again, by making either a mental or a written note.

Sum up

Finally, to sum up the experiment, and think about what you have learned, compare your answers to the two sets of questions. Draw some conclusions about what happened, first about the effects of focusing your attention on yourself, and second about the effects of focusing your attention on others.

- What did you do in order to use your curiosity, and focus on other people?

- How did you do it?

- Could you do it again, in more demanding situations?

Doing a brief two-way mini-experiment when talking to someone is particularly helpful. You may need to carry out a few two-way experiments to gain the maximum

The two-way experiment worksheet

Step 1. Focus on yourself for three to five minutes.

(a) Notice everything that is going on inside you. For example, notice all the sensations that you can feel; how cold or hot you are; whether you are hungry, or tired, or full of aches and pains. Notice how your clothes feel on your body. Notice your feelings, and any thoughts, images, impressions or memories that come to mind.

(b) Answer the assessment questions (write your answers down):

1 How did you feel when focusing on yourself? _____

2 What did you notice? Write down as much as you can here.

_____

_____

Step 2. Focus on things outside yourself for three to five minutes.

(a) Notice other people: how they look, what they are wearing, what they might be feeling or thinking about.

(b) Answer the two assessment questions (write your answers down):

1 How did you feel when focusing outside yourself? _____

2 What did you notice? Write down as much as you can here.

_____

_____

Step 3. Compare the two.

What was different?_____

What was the same?_____

Step 4. Summarize your conclusions: **Self focus**   **Other focus**

Which made you feel better?

_____

Which gave you more of the information
that helps you along socially?

_____

Was focusing on other people difficult to achieve?
How did you do it?

_____

Do you need more practice to achieve the
desired effect?

benefit from them. Rather like pulling a pendulum back before swinging it in the other direction, this experiment allows you to compare two extreme ways of paying attention. In the end you might find a mid-point of attention-focusing, allowing your attention to come and to go more naturally and freely.

Making use of observation: curiosity in practice

If you went to the departures gate at an airport you would see lots of people saying goodbye to each other. At the arrivals gate you would see another lot of people meeting up and greeting each other. As a curious observer of people in this setting you would notice that there are many different ways of parting and greeting. What happens depends on many things:

- The age of the people

- How well they know each other

- Their nationality

- Their moods

- How long they will be, or have been, apart

- Who else is with them and so on.

There is clearly no single or right way of saying hello and goodbye, even though this is one of the most basic of all social interactions.

But shy people, and people who are socially anxious, often talk as if they were in danger of 'doing it wrong' – as if there was an ideal way to behave. They also assume that what they do will fall short of this ideal, and therefore run the risk of being 'unacceptable'.

But whose way of behaving is the ideal? At the airport we can see that either ideals are very different between people or that the range of acceptable practice is much wider than anxious people suppose it is.

In the end people do whatever they feel comfortable with, or what works for them. This is why there is no need to be self-conscious about the way you do things.

If there are no absolute ideals for how we should behave, moment by moment, with each other, then there is no reason to suppose that doing something in an unusual way, or in a way that feels wrong, attracts the attention of others.

It's worth remembering...

- Usually symptoms of social anxiety feel worse than they look. When you think everyone can see the shaking or nervousness that you can feel, you are usually wrong.
- Even when people do notice, they usually pay little attention, as it does not have much significance for them.
- You may look calm even when you do not feel calm.
- Most people do not notice much about what others do. They are more likely to be preoccupied with their own concerns.
- Most people do not spend much time judging, criticizing or evaluating others.
- Practically no one is completely happy with the way they are, or with the way they get on with others.

Opposite effects of social anxiety

One of the odd things about social anxiety is that it produces a number of effects that are often the opposite to each other. Let's take a look at some of them. You might want to place a tick beside any you relate to.

1   You may feel as if you are the centre of attention. At the same time you may feel so inferior and inadequate that you believe that no one is at all interested in you.

2   You may become preoccupied with yourself and with what is happening to you, and experience painful bouts of self-consciousness. At the same time you may be quite uncertain about your identity – about who you are.

3   You want to do things right, and to be acceptable. But you still want your individuality to be recognized and to be able to realize your potential.

4   You do not want to be disregarded. But you want to be invisible.

5   You think you are not worth noticing. But you are quite sure that everyone notices you.

6   You want to keep the bad feelings in check. But you find it hard to stop doing things that make the bad feelings worse.

Some people, noticing these opposite or paradoxical effects, think that being socially anxious is a kind of self-importance. They think that it is based on the assumption that you matter so much that everyone pays, or should pay, you lots of attention.

In fact, social anxiety is more often based on the opposite assumption. Many sufferers believe that they are in some way weak, inferior, inadequate or less good than others. This is combined with the fear that this inferiority will be noticed and will prevent you getting on with people and feeling that you belong.

Learning the techniques for reducing self-consciousness is one way in which you can discover for yourself that you possess all the qualities you need right now to form happy and positive relationships with other people. You just need to build your confidence and express the real you.

Self-consciousness and keeping safe

When you are overtaken by a bout of self-consciousness it can be extremely difficult to turn your attention away from yourself. That is why we've provided the practical suggestions above to help you do it. That's also why you need to practise by first focusing your attention outside yourself in situations that are not too threatening.

There is another explanation for why it can be difficult to put the suggestions in this section into effect. The inward focus that goes with self-consciousness, and which increases the longer it continues, can be another way of protecting yourself. It can feel as if you dare not focus your attention on the outside world, for fear of what you might find out there – as if you were fearful of picking up other people's negative signals and judgements.

This fear makes it hard to turn your attention outwards: to look straight at someone when you know you are about to blush, or think you have made a fool of yourself in some way. You don't want to let them see you 'at your worst', and have to watch their reactions when they spot your vulnerability. It is easier to glance briefly up and then look away, retreating into yourself again, than to give up the self-protection altogether.

But brief ventures into the outside world in this way tend to increase your fear rather than to reduce it. They alert you to the possibility of danger out there without giving you long enough to assess its reality or to think about how to defuse it.

Why self-protection doesn't work

These self-protective attempts of focusing in on your own thoughts and feelings are understandable, but they fail. They won't protect you because they reduce your curiosity and make it impossible to challenge your fears.

Focusing on your own feelings and thoughts affects what you notice, and therefore the information that gets into your mind. It also affects the way you interpret the information that you have noticed, and influences how you think about it. And it determines the kind of information that you store about what happened, so it also affects what you remember afterwards.

In this section we've focused on how to change what you notice: how to make sure that you keep in touch with what is really happening and do not deprive yourself of accurate information about the world outside yourself.

It's worth remembering...

Self-consciousness, focusing your attention on to your inner experiences, fills your mind with information that tends to make you feel worse.

In later sections we'll look at how changing your patterns of thinking and behaviour can also help reduce self-consciousness. Reducing negative thinking patterns can help you do things differently and to become socially involved with people in more spontaneous, less self-conscious ways.

Summary

1 Self-consciousness comes from focusing your attention inwards.

2 It is at the centre of all the vicious cycles that help to keep social anxiety going.

3 It also makes social anxiety worse.

4 Focusing attention inwards fills you with information about yourself and your reactions to feeling anxious. It also means that you have less attention available for things outside yourself. So feeling self-conscious leaves you short of accurate, detailed information. It leaves you with a hazy impression of what was going on.

5 Reducing self-consciousness involves: working out how self-consciousness affects you; deciding not to think about how bad you are feeling; filling your mind with something else.

6 It is extremely helpful to use your sense of curiosity. Think of yourself as a scientist who is finding out more about social interactions. You could carry out two-way experiments, in easy situations first; and you could turn yourself into an accurate, interested and curious observer.

7 It may take some courage to stop retreating into yourself, and instead to focus on what is happening around you. Although the retreat feels safer, it can make you vulnerable to episodes of self-consciousness. Facing the world is a far safer option in the end.

8 Self-consciousness influences what you notice, how you interpret it and what you remember. Broadening your focus of attention changes what you notice.

SECTION 3: Changing Thinking Patterns

This section will help you understand:

- How to find out what you are thinking
- Patterns of biased thinking
- How to find different ways of thinking
- How to handle upsetting thoughts
- How to handle pressurizing thoughts
- How to handle extremist thoughts
- What to do when thinking patterns are difficult to change
- How to remember new patterns of thinking.

Looking at kinds of thoughts

Thoughts, feelings and behaviour influence each other all the time to keep social anxiety going. The case study below reveals the many ways in which patterns of thinking can affect people who are socially anxious or shy.

Read the case study carefully and count the number of thinking patterns you can find. Only some of them are described as thoughts.

CASE STUDY

Imagine you arrive at a friend's house for a meal and find the room full of people you do not know. There is a pause in the conversation as you walk in and you think: 'Everyone is looking at me.' This makes you nervous, so you leap at the offer of a drink but feel hot and conspicuous when someone asks you your name. You think: 'They must all have noticed how nervous I am', as you avoid catching anyone's eye and look round for somewhere to put your drink down in case it spills.

You wonder if you will ever be able to think of anything to say and start to feel uncomfortably hot. The louder people talk the more you think 'I really don't belong here', and 'Nothing I could think of to say would interest these people'. This makes it harder for you to join in the conversation, so you keep quiet and retreat into your shell, aware of how inept you must seem in other people's eyes. You look out for a way of leaving early, hoping that you can slip away without drawing too much attention to yourself.

The next day you can't stop thinking about how you must have appeared to the other people there. Images come to mind that bring back all the embarrassment and nervousness that you felt at the time. You decide you will never do that sort of thing again.

Other thoughts also go through your mind, about how hard it is to make friends, and how inadequate you feel compared to other people. You wonder if you can ever change, as you have always been shy. Other shy people seem to have managed to grow out of it, so you also ask yourself whether there is something wrong with you. The longer this train of thoughts goes on the more dispirited and the sadder you feel.

In this case study:

- wondering

- deciding

- becoming aware of yourself

- having images

are all types of thinking patterns.

The last paragraph of the case study shows how one thought leads on to another in an increasingly distressing stream which reflects the meaning to you of what happened.

Different kinds of thoughts

You may have noticed your thoughts, and the way that they can make you feel anxious and affect how you feel and what you do. Or you may hardly have noticed them at all.

When your thoughts go unnoticed this may be partly because thoughts are of many different kinds, and partly because there is often no reason to express them in words. This is not something that people usually ask you to do. What's more, putting your thoughts into words can sometimes provoke the feelings that go with the thoughts, and make you feel worse. Nobody really wants to think about exactly how foolish they appeared.

Nevertheless, it is important to know about the different types of thoughts so that you will be more likely to recognize them when you have them. Thoughts include:

- ideas, expectations and attitudes;

- they may come as images, impressions or memories;

- they may be beliefs and assumptions or 'rules for living' that go without saying.

All of these ways of thinking reflect what goes on in your mind in different ways, and they can all play a part in the vicious cycles that keep social anxiety going. This is true even if you are not fully aware of some of your thoughts, and even if you do not usually put them into words, or recognize them as 'thoughts'.

Examples of kinds of thoughts

Thoughts can be like **half-formed ideas**, for instance about being different from other people without being able to say exactly how.

Thoughts may be reflected in **images or impressions** of yourself which come from an earlier stage of life. These could be based on memories of a particularly painful experience, such as being rejected or bullied, or singled out for criticism.

Many people, for example, report suddenly feeling small when confronted by unexpected criticism, or by someone in authority over them. They also describe having related images, such as an image of themselves as a child facing up to a large and critical teacher. Often such images have something in common with what is happening in the present, even when the person who has them cannot immediately recognize what this is. (We looked at this in more detail in Part One, Section 5, page 62.)

Expectations like expecting to be judged are common in people who are socially anxious. Having an expectation can be more like having an attitude that influences the way you think about things, than having a thought.

Negative beliefs, for example about being inadequate or incompetent or unacceptable, often go with low self-confidence ('I can't ever seem to do things right'). Thinking this way also reveals a lack of belief in yourself.

You may have beliefs about other people as well as yourself. For example, you may believe that everyone is always watching out for other people's failings and noticing their shortcomings. Or you may believe that everyone is more confident and competent than you are.

If this is what you believe, then you may have developed assumptions and rules for living that fit with this belief, such as:

- 'If you do something stupid people will criticize and reject you'

- 'Never stick your neck out. Make sure you keep yourself well in the background'.

These are all ways of thinking, and some of them are harder to recognize than others.

The main strategies for changing thinking patterns

This section describes the main strategies for dealing with thoughts that make you feel bad, and that help to keep your social anxiety going. There are two steps:

1 Learning how to identify what is in your mind; what you are thinking.

2 Learning how to re-examine the ways you think.

Your problem may seem to be confusing, and you may find it difficult to disentangle its different aspects. The straightforward examples in the rest of this section will help you to learn what to do, and start you moving in the right direction.

   This section focuses on thought patterns that are relatively easy to recognize. There will be some here that are relevant to everyone – even those people who are only rarely socially anxious. Section 2 of Part Three focuses on the types of underlying assumptions and beliefs that can make it hard to build up more confidence in yourself socially. They can slow down your progress if you do not make a special effort to change them also.

   These strategies will help you learn how to tune in to your thoughts and then to take another look at them. The way you are currently thinking is keeping your social anxiety going. It is what you are thinking that explains why particular situations seem to be 'socially dangerous' – to be risky or threatening. Finding another way of seeing things will make you feel better and be more helpful to you.

Step 1: Find out what you are thinking

The first step is to become aware of what runs through your mind when you feel tense or anxious. This is easier said than done because the sorts of thoughts – and images – that make anxiety worse are often difficult to identify. They come and go quickly, and may also have become automatic. They are like bad habits: you may not be fully aware of them because they are so familiar, as if you had been looking through coloured spectacles without knowing that they were there.

   Think now about a recent situation in which you felt socially anxious. Perhaps it was a party, a work social event or during a meeting. When you can remember the situation quite clearly, try to answer the key questions opposite.

We've provided a worked example below to get you started.

The situation

A meeting at work. I had to present an idea to the group.

Key questions for Step 1: identifying your thoughts

What went through your mind when you started to feel anxious? And after that? And when it was all over?

I thought my colleagues would think my idea was nothing new or original and that I was making a fool of myself. I started to feel really stupid, embarrassed and nervous. I thought they were noticing I was blushing and looking nervous and that made me feel still more nervous. An image popped into my head of having to do a presentation to the class at school and stammering. Everyone had laughed at me then and I can still remember how awful I had felt – humiliated, an idiot. After the meeting I thought I'd confirmed my colleagues' worst opinion of me and I'd never be asked to present anything again. And if I was asked I'd definitely refuse anyway because it had been so traumatic.

What was the worst thing that might have happened at the time?

People could have laughed out loud at my idea.

What is it about this situation that matters to you?

It matters because I looked so foolish in front of colleagues and because I wasn't able to be professional or even just normal. Other people can do that kind of thing.

What does having this experience mean to you?

It's proof of my incompetence and failure.

What does it mean about you?

I'm inadequate; I'm hopeless at any kind of social situation.

Did any of your thoughts make you feel worse? If so, which ones?

I felt worse the more I thought about what other people might be noticing about my behaviour or thinking about me.

Now answer the questions for yourself with a particular personal situation in mind.

The situation:

_____

1 What went through your mind when you started to feel anxious? And after that? And when it was all over?

_____

_____

_____

_____

2 What was the worst thing that might have happened at the time?

_____

_____

_____

3 What is it about this situation that matters to you?

_____

_____

_____

4 What does having this experience mean to you?

_____

_____

_____

5 What does it mean about you?

_____

_____

_____

_____

6 Did any of your thoughts make you feel worse? If so, which ones?

_____

_____

_____

_____

Linking thoughts and feelings

When identifying the thoughts that are important and relevant for you, look for those that fit with the way you felt. Sometimes it is easy to make this fit: if you felt embarrassed and remember thinking that you might have offended someone by mistake, then this obviously seems to fit. Sometimes it is much harder.

For example, you might have felt totally rejected, even though nothing that you can remember seems to have provoked that feeling. When this happens, keep asking yourself the key questions. Try to stand back from the problem far enough to identify your personal perspective on it. Maybe the powerful feeling (for example, a sense of being rejected) reflects one of your attitudes or beliefs, or particular memories that you have. Thinking about what the situation means to you and why it matters to you helps to identify these thoughts.

Using the thought record

The 'Thought record for identifying thoughts' shown overleaf is a useful way to pinpoint your thoughts. It will also help you to separate them from the feelings that went with them. An example of a completed form has also been provided. Extra blank copies are provided at the back of the book.

Writing things down is a good way of developing the habit of recognizing what you are thinking, and noticing how your thoughts influence the way that you feel.

Thought record for identifying thoughts: *example*

Situation (be specific)	Feelings (there may be more than one)	Thoughts, impressions, etc. (keep the different thoughts separate)
The boss asks to see me	Nervous Worried	He thinks my work is no good
Left alone with an attractive person	Terrified Miserable	I'm making a fool of myself Nobody likes me much
Going out with friends to the pub	Panicky Shaky Heart racing	They'll think I'm odd I can't tell jokes
A neighbour drops in	Embarrassed	I can't relax and be normal
Remembering being stuck for words	Flustered Mortified	I'm useless I can't do things right
Thought I'd say the wrong thing	Ashamed Fearful Heart racing	I'm as red as is humanly possible
A colleague got angry with me	Humiliated Rejected	Feel small and insignificant, like I did at school

Thought record for identifying thoughts

Situation (be specific)	Feelings (there may be more than one)	Thoughts, impressions, etc. (keep the different thoughts separate)

Keep a record for a few days of situations in which you feel anxious or upset. Always start by thinking of specific situations or incidents that happened to you recently, and that you remember well. Use these as cues to help put into words the things that go through your mind when you are anxious: the thoughts, ideas, attitudes, images and so on, as in the examples provided. Refer to the key questions above and use them as prompts. Note down:

- Details of the situation; what it was and when it occurred

- What feelings you experienced (e.g. fear, anxiety, fed up, shaky)

- Your thoughts, or what was in your mind when you felt that way.

Your aim at this stage should be to pay close attention to your thoughts when you feel anxious or upset. See if you can put into words the things that go through your mind, as in the examples shown in the table.

You may find this difficult if it seems to you that the anxiety just comes 'out of the blue', without there being any thoughts behind it. If that is the case try doing something that makes you feel anxious, just so that you can pay special attention to the thoughts that run through your mind when you do.

Another option is to ask yourself the key questions about what the situation means about you, or means to you. Answering these questions may help you put some of your attitudes and expectations into words. These are not like thoughts that run through your mind at the time, but they are still thought processes. They can have a significant impact on the way you feel, and on what you do when confronted by a difficult situation.

Be accurate

It is important to be as accurate in observing your feelings and thoughts as you can, and it is easy to forget. So use this workbook and keep it to hand as far as possible. Get into a habit of making a mental note of what happens and writing it down as soon as you can. If you always start by thinking about specific situations, about things that have happened to you quite recently, you will find it easier to identify the thoughts. This is because you will know where in your memory to start looking for them.

It is important not to just dwell on the feelings themselves, but to use them to prompt you to think about your thinking. Doing this exercise is like becoming an expert mechanic who listens to the sound of the engine, watches how the car performs, and then tunes in to possible sources of trouble.

When it's hard to work out why you feel the way you do

Sometimes you feel bad – anxious, nervous or embarrassed, for example – apparently for no reason at all. However, there always is a reason; it just may be difficult to work out what it is. The thoughts come and go quickly, and attitudes and beliefs do not have to be put into words to influence how you feel.

Think about any memories, fleeting images or general impressions that occurred when you felt anxious. This often helps in understanding why you felt so bad at the time. It may help you to recognize how your thoughts – what happens in your mind – keep the problem going. If you had an image of being yelled at in public and wanting to run away and hide, it would not be surprising to feel distressed and conspicuous. Such impressions may continue to influence the present even though they really belong in the past. Also images provoke strong feelings, so they tend to keep the vicious cycle of thoughts and feelings spinning.

Patterns of biased thinking

Different kinds of thoughts typically occur before, during and after the situation that caused you problems.

Before the event

Before the event you may make **predictions**: predicting that you will do or say something wrong, or in some way reveal your 'inadequacy'.

During the event

During the event many people go in for **mind reading**, or guessing how other people are reacting to them and what they are thinking. Or they **catastrophize**, and assume that what happened was far worse than it really was.

After the event

Afterwards it can be difficult to stop dwelling on what you think went wrong, judging and criticizing yourself and making assumptions about how you came across and how others reacted – like doing a **post mortem**.

These are all what therapists call **biased ways of thinking**. They are biased thoughts because they are influenced by your habit of taking an anxious perspective on things.

They are therefore likely to be inaccurate. Like looking through a pair of distorting spectacles, these ways of thinking are especially likely to be associated with misperceptions and misinterpretations about what is really happening, as well as with feeling bad.

Getting rid of the bias and getting your thoughts back in perspective will make you feel better, but first you need to recognize that the bias is there.

Common forms of biased thinking

We've listed some common forms of bias below, together with some examples of the thoughts that might go with them. Most of us tend to think in favourite ways. This may help to explain why we readily fall into patterns of thinking.

If you can identify your favourite ways of thinking, you will be in a better position to spot the thinking bias in action: 'There I go again – mind reading or guessing what other people are thinking', for example. If you can do this you will have made a major step in overcoming your social anxiety.

Taking things personally

This involves supposing that somebody else's actions were directed, personally, towards you: for example, when someone leaves the room or looks away while you are talking.

Have you done this recently? Describe what happened here.

_____

_____

_____

_____

Taking the blame

This involves taking responsibility for something when it is not yours. For example, 'He was really angry. It must be my fault. I wonder what I can do to make it better?'

Have you done this recently? Describe what happened here.

_____

_____

_____

_____

Mind reading

This involves believing that you know what others are thinking. For example, 'She thinks I'm not talkative enough'; 'He doesn't like people who are shy'; 'They know just how hopeless I am at this'.

Have you done this recently? Describe what happened here.

_____

_____

_____

_____

Discounting the positive

This involves rejecting good things as if they did not count (or using a negative filter). For example, 'She only said that to make me feel better'; 'Anybody should be able to order a meal. Doing that OK is no big deal'; 'They were just being polite'.

Have you done this recently? Describe what happened here.

_____

_____

_____

_____

Emotional reasoning

This involves mistaking feelings for facts: 'I'm so embarrassed, I know everyone is looking at me'. It involves supposing you are inadequate because that's the way you feel.

Have you done this recently? Describe what happened here.

_____

_____

_____

_____

Catastrophizing

This involves thinking that if something goes wrong it will be a disaster: 'If I put a foot wrong this relationship is totally doomed'; 'If this goes badly I will never be able to show my face here again'.

Have you done this recently? Describe what happened here.

_____

_____

_____

_____

Over-generalizing

This involves assuming that because something happened once, this means it will always happen: for example, because you spilled a drink, or failed to see a joke, you will always do something clumsy or miss the point.

Have you done this recently? Describe what happened here.

_____

_____

_____

_____

Predicting the future, or fortune telling

Examples of this include thinking things such as 'I'll never be able to feel comfortable talking to someone attractive'; 'I'll always be on my own'; 'Nobody will ever invite me along'.

Have you done this recently? Describe what happened here.

_____

_____

_____

_____

Labelling, or name-calling

This involves giving yourself a hard time; for example, thinking things such as 'I'm useless … inept … stupid … inferior'; 'Other people are unfriendly … critical … hostile … superior'.

Have you done this recently? Describe what happened here.

_____

_____

_____

_____

Wishful thinking

This involves supposing things would be better if they were different. 'If only I were cleverer … more attractive … wittier … younger … more like others.'

Have you done this recently? Describe what happened here.

_____

_____

_____

_____

Can you now work out which types of thinking you do most often? Write them down here.

_____

_____

_____

_____

_____

Step 2: Looking for alternative ways of thinking

Looking for alternative ways of thinking is one of the main things you can do to make yourself feel better. The rest of this section explains how to do this using pencil and paper, and how to do it in your head. More methods are also described in the next sections on doing things differently and building up confidence. All these strategies can be used to help you to rethink your attitudes to your social life, your assumptions about it, and the way that you approach it.

Once you know what you are thinking, the next step is to re-examine your thoughts. The aim is to learn to question your thoughts, rather than accept them as facts. Explore them, and the things that spring to mind when you think about them. See whether they fit together, make sense and are helpful to you.

When you do this you will find that there is no one right way of seeing things. Rather, there are many possibilities. Some can make you feel worse, and others can make you feel better.

Let's look at a practical example to make this clearer. Imagine you are having a meal with a number of other people. You might think that everyone else is doing things right, but you are doing them wrong. Thinking this way will probably make you feel tense and nervous about what you say and do, and very self-conscious. As a result it becomes hard to relax or to eat, or to think of anything else.

However, there are other ways of thinking about the same situation. Here are some of the other options:

- Everyone is doing some things 'right' and some things 'wrong'

- Nobody but you is thinking in terms of right and wrong anyway

- There are so many different ways of doing things that it matters little which you choose

- People are more interested in what you think than in whether you do things the 'right' way

- Doing things differently from others makes people curious about you, but nothing more than that.

The point is that there is a far wider choice of ways of thinking than springs to mind at first. You could see the clouds in the sky as a sign of rain, and feel disappointed. Or you could see them as a chance of sunshine and feel altogether more cheerful. There are many other options as well.

The way you think, and what you choose to think about will affect the way you feel.

> ### It's worth remembering...
>
> **Learning how to think things through gives you more control over the way you feel.**

For example, someone who thought,

'They think I'm peculiar'

would be likely to feel unhappy or rejected.

They might feel less upset if instead they asked themselves,

'How do I know what they are thinking?'

and then answered that question with the new thought,

'Maybe I'm just guessing. I may be no odder than lots of people.'

Often socially anxious people are making guesses such as this one, and jumping to conclusions about what others think of them.

What would you think if someone you knew well but had not seen for a while passed close by to you in the street but did not even smile? Would you think something like, 'I must have done something to offend them', or 'I don't suppose they really like me'? If so, this is a good example of the kind of guesswork that ties in with the fear that others will think badly about you, but which is not based on the facts of what happened. Stop and think for a minute about what you would really think in this situation. Write down your ideas here.

_____

_____

_____

_____

_____

_____

Questioning your upsetting thoughts

You can learn to find alternatives to upsetting thoughts such as those described above by asking yourself some more key questions.

Let's look at a worked example first and see how the questions apply to a recent event Sally, who suffers from social anxiety, found upsetting.

Key questions for Step 2: Looking for alternatives

The event:

Sally is 50 and married with two grown-up children. She's always kept to herself but since both her children left home she's found herself increasingly lonely and feeling isolated. She's been invited to a neighbour's barbecue and after nearly backing out several times through shyness, decides at last to go.

Unfortunately when she arrives she finds she doesn't know many people there very well and feels very nervous and shy. She spots a woman who she knows from the local neighbourhood watch group she belongs to. Marie has always been quite chatty and friendly in the past and had asked her over for coffee a few times. In turn Sally has babysat Marie's 10-year-old child and been supportive when Marie was under pressure and needed time out.

Sally decides to go over to speak to Marie but after they've exchange a couple of sentences Marie says she has to get back home to check on her family and leaves abruptly. Sally feels hurt and rejected and decides what she had to say must have been very boring. What's more she decides that Marie must never have liked her very much in the first place.

What are the facts?

What evidence does Sally have to support what she thinks? What evidence is there against it? Which way of thinking fits best with the facts? The fact that you think something does not make it true.

The evidence to support Sally's view that Marie thinks she's boring and has never liked her is that a short time after talking to her Marie leaves. The evidence against this is that Marie explained she had to go and check on her family and this may have been true; also Marie has been friendly and chatty in the past. There seems more evidence to support the view that Marie does like Sally and simply couldn't stay any longer at the party because of other commitments.

What possible alternatives are there?

What would Sally think if she were more confident? How might someone else view this situation? What would you say to someone else who was thinking in this sort of way? What would someone who cared about you say?

If she were more confident Sally might think that she is an interesting and nice person and that she and Marie have always got on well in the past. The fact that Marie has to leave is not a direct insult. Another person at the party might observe that Marie is a very busy woman who takes her role as mother very seriously. They might know that one of her children is not well and even though Marie's husband is looking after the children Marie already feels she's stayed too long. Someone else might observe that Sally seems overly sensitive and perhaps is being unfair to Marie. Someone who cared for Sally might say that she is being overly hard on herself, imagining that she is being boring.

What is the worst possible way of seeing things, or the worst thing that could possibly happen?

What is the best way of seeing things, or the best thing that could happen? Which is most realistic? Or most likely to be right?

The worst way of seeing things is that Sally is right, Marie has never liked her and was just being polite all those other times. The worst thing that could happen is that Marie actually says this to other people behind Sally's back and that absolutely no one likes Sally.

The best way of seeing things is that Marie had to get back to her child and was sorry not to be able to spend more time with Sally. The best thing that could happen is that Marie invites her over for a morning coffee and a proper catch-up soon.

It's not realistic that Marie has just been polite all these times because she's actually gone out of her way to maintain contact with Sally and invite her to do things together. What's more, Sally was invited to the neighbour's barbecue so that's evidence that other people like Sally as well and that she is a likable person.

What biases might be affecting Sally's thinking?

For example, is she jumping to conclusions? Exaggerating? Over-generalizing? Is she predicting the future as a certainty? Or mind reading? Or focusing on the negative side of things at the expense of everything else?

Sally jumps to the conclusion that Marie leaves suddenly because she finds Sally boring. She exaggerates the importance of Marie leaving and takes it personally. She overgeneralizes from the fact that Marie left that Marie has never liked her and engages in mind-reading that this is what Marie actually thinks. She focuses on the negative fact that Marie left rather than remembering all the other times Marie has actively sought out her company.

What could Sally do that would be helpful?

What personal skills and strengths does she have to help? What past experience of dealing with similar problems? What help, advice and support is available to her, from others or from books? What can she do to change things? If she can't change the situation, could she keep an open mind about what it means?

Sally is a kind person who has given Marie support in the past. She could use her resources as a supportive and more experienced parent to overcome her fear that Marie doesn't like her and ask Marie if she can help look after her children. Sally could talk to other neighbours and check how Marie is getting along and whether she needs help. Sally could change things by spending more time with Marie (and other friends) so that she feels more confident about herself and what she has to offer as a friend. She could certainly keep an open mind that this one occasion does not prove that Marie actually dislikes her.

Now think about a recent situation you found upsetting and answer these same questions.

Answering your upsetting thoughts

Use these questions constantly to help you to rethink, and keep writing your answers down, so that you do not forget them. After you have gotten used to asking yourself the detailed questions you may find it easier to use the simple two-column thought record shown on page 64. There are extra blank versions of this form at the back of the book.

The aim is to search your mind for other ways of thinking. It's important, however, to recognize that these may not come easily at first. We've provided some examples in the table. We've also left a space for you to use, if you wish, to re-examine your thoughts about being ignored by someone who knows you well. Can you find another way of thinking about it?

Key Questions

Alternative ways of thinking

The event:

_____

_____

What are the facts?
What evidence do you have to support what you think? What evidence is there against it? Which way of thinking fits best with the facts? The fact that you think something does not make it true.

_____

_____

What possible alternatives are there?
What would you think if you were more confident? How might someone else view this situation? What would you say to someone else who was thinking in this sort of way? What would someone who cared about you say?

_____

_____

What is the worst possible way of seeing things, or the worst thing that could possibly happen?
What is the best way of seeing things, or the best thing that could happen? Which is most realistic? Or most likely to be right?

_____

_____

What biases might be affecting your thinking?
For example, are you jumping to conclusions? Exaggerating? Over-generalizing? Are you predicting the future as a certainty? Or mind reading? Or focusing on the negative side of things at the expense of everything else?

_____

_____

What could you do that would be helpful?
What personal skills and strengths do you have to help? What past experience of dealing with similar problems? What help, advice and support is available to you, from others or from books? What can you do to change things? If you can't change the situation, could you keep an open mind about what it means?

_____

_____

Sometimes people think they can re-examine their thoughts without writing things down – doing it in their heads – and, indeed, sometimes they are right. Nevertheless, for everyone it is important to do this exercise in writing enough times to be sure that you really can identify alternative ways of thinking and put them into words. Otherwise it is tempting to be satisfied with a rather vague notion of having achieved a different way of seeing things. Vague ideas are less likely to have a beneficial effect on how you feel than ones that are clearer. Putting the new ideas into words by completing a thought record like the one below brings them into focus.

Thought record for looking for alternatives: *example*

Upsetting thoughts (take one at a time)	Possible alternatives (there may be more than one)
I sound really stupid	Perhaps everyone does once in a while Even if I did, it would not mean I was stupid
They can see how nervous I am	Possible, but that needn't make them think I'm a bad person. Maybe they are thinking of other things altogether, and have not even noticed me
That person completely ignored me	

The important thing while you're thinking of alternatives is to keep an open mind, and not to get led astray by your fears. These tend to push you into extreme positions such as thinking: 'Everyone could see that I made a complete idiot of myself'. Instead the aim of the exercise is to lead you towards a more balanced, and usually more accurate, way of seeing things. Here are some examples of more balanced thinking:

- 'Maybe people are not judging or evaluating me, or even noticing me particularly.'

- 'Maybe I can't tell what people are really thinking.'

- 'Maybe I feel worse than I look.'

- 'Maybe people don't reject you for being nervous – after all, it happens to everyone sometimes.'

- 'Maybe I'm just as good as they are, underneath.'

Thought record for looking for alternatives

Upsetting thoughts	Possible alternatives

Give yourself the benefit of the doubt. Try to think as you might if you had none of the bad feelings that have sent you in search of help. Take yourself on a mind-trip, and see if you can find other perspectives to explore.

Finding 'good' alternatives

Good alternative ways of thinking come in many shapes and sizes. You are the best person to judge which ones will work for you. A good alternative is one that:

- Makes you feel better

- Fits with the facts (not with your fears or suspicions, or with a biased interpretation of the facts)

- Helps you to do the things that you want to do.

Look at the alternatives that you find alongside the overcoming social anxiety goals that you set yourself to begin with (see page 6). Ask yourself whether the new way of thinking would help you to achieve those goals.

Good alternatives also help you to break old patterns of thinking like the biases listed earlier. Watch out for your favourites, and see if you can spot them in action at times when you feel bad. You might find yourself saying something like: 'There I go, discounting the positive things again.'

Unlike biased ways of thinking (especially catastrophizing, or over-generalizing), helpful alternatives can usually be expressed in moderate or 'open-minded' language, as in the 'maybe' examples listed above. They make you feel less pressurized, and help you to adopt a balanced and flexible view of things rather than an extremist one.

Pressurizing thoughts

Examples of pressurizing thoughts include:

- 'I **must** think of something interesting to say.'

- 'I **should** be able to like people more.'

- 'I **ought** to try harder to be amusing and entertaining.'

Pressurizing thoughts contain pressurizing words, like **must**, **should** and **ought**. Many people use these words to motivate themselves, or to urge themselves on to do better and to 'improve'. In the end they work against you because the pressure adds to the tension and anxiety. They also suggest that there are definite rules that you must obey rather than various sets of social conventions which have grown up gradually and that in practice are frequently broken. Think of the people you know who break the conventions but do not worry about it.

Looking for less pressurizing alternatives may feel uncomfortable at first, as if something bad might happen if you did not do what you 'ought' to do. One way round this problem is to try thinking in terms of preferences, not pressures. Prompt yourself with: 'It would be better if ...', rather than push yourself with 'must', 'should' or 'ought'.

List here some of the pressurizing thoughts you use about yourself and try to write a less pressurizing alternative. We've started you off.

Pressurizing thought: *I must socialize more at work.*
Alternative: *I'll try to chat to people from time to time when I feel able and ready.*

Pressurizing thought:

Alternative:

Pressurizing thought:

Alternative:

Pressurizing thought:

Alternative:

_____

_____

Extremist thoughts

Extremist thoughts contain extreme words such as **always, never, totally, nobody** and so on. Examples of extremist thoughts are:

- 'They **totally** ignored me.'

- 'People **never** like me.'

- 'I am **always** messing things up.'

- '**Nobody** feels shy after the age of 30.'

By their very nature, extremist statements are most unlikely to be true. Perhaps they could be true, but it would be worth taking notice if this happened: like being able to run a four-minute mile, or meeting someone as clever as Einstein.

List here some of the extremist thoughts you have about yourself and your social anxiety. Are they true when you really examine them?

_____

_____

_____

_____

Sometimes the pressurizing and the extremist words come together. Here are some examples:

- 'You should always be polite.'

- 'I should never show that I am angry.'

- 'You must always let other people come first.'

These statements are like rules for living, and they tie in closely with the underlying beliefs and assumptions that everyone absorbs as they grow up. In some circumstances they make sense – and these examples illustrate well the kinds of things that parents and teachers tend to say, and the kinds of 'rules' they may try to incorporate into the home or the classroom.

However, we are all at times impolite, angry and in pursuit of our own goals. We often want to do things our own way irrespective of what others want. So, instead of combining the pressure and the extremism when this happens – and hitting yourself with a 'double whammy' – it helps again to look for more balanced and moderate ways of seeing things. Instead of using phrases that sound like hidden threats – as if there were an unspoken 'or else …' behind them – look for more helpful alternatives. Threats work less well than rewards when you are learning something new, and they also add to feelings of nervousness, apprehension and anxiety.

Some of the options might be:

- 'Things often work out better if you can be polite.'

- 'Everyone gets angry at times – but it does make a difference how you show it.'

- 'It's perfectly all right for me to come first at times.'

Can you see how these more balanced alternatives point the way forwards? They define the kinds of strategies that it can be helpful to develop, such as ways of negotiating differences, expressing anger and taking turns.

Do you sometimes think in both pressurizing and extremist ways? Write down some examples here and then try to find a more balanced alternative.

_____

_____

_____

_____

What makes searching for alternatives difficult?

'Yes, but …'

Being anxious goes with worrying about what might happen next; about what else could possibly go wrong, and about how bad it would be if it did. This makes it easy to doubt any new perspectives, and to follow each one up with a 'Yes, but …' as we can see in the following examples:

- 'Yes, I know they seemed to like me, but they don't really know what I'm like.'

- 'Yes, I didn't say anything stupid, but then I hardly said anything at all.'

Doubting is another way of discounting, and the way to overcome it is to use the strategies of cognitive therapy: identify the discounting thought and re-examine it, to see if it really makes sense.

So in the first example above, a way of re-examining your thought could be to say: '**Maybe** people cannot tell what I am really like until they get to know me better.'

And in the second example, you could say:
'**Maybe** saying more, and taking more initiative when I am talking to people, would be a fairer test of my thought about appearing stupid.'

List some of the 'Yes, but' thoughts you have about any successes you've had with managing your social anxiety. Write a more balanced alternative here.

_____

_____

_____

_____

The inner critic

Another difficulty with finding alternatives arises when you pay too much attention to the internal voice that:

- Puts you down

- Deals out criticism

- Hands out the blame when things appear not to go well.

All of us can have an inner conversation with ourselves at times. It's as if we were talking to another self: 'you fool' we say – as if we did not know that we'd made a mistake or done something stupid quite well already.

This internal monologue, or dialogue, tends to incorporate messages that we have heard elsewhere. Sometimes it has recognizable characteristics of our parents, teachers or friends: 'If you don't speak up, no wonder people can't hear what you say'. Sometimes it reflects our own self-opinion: 'You're useless'.

The trouble with this internal voice is that it comes from inside, and is far more likely to reflect opinion than fact. Once again the answer is to stick to the facts, and not to be misled by some outdated ways of thinking that may have little to do with the present, and which make you feel bad.

Feeling low

Feeling discouraged, demoralized or depressed also makes it hard to see things another way. It is as if your black mood colours the way you see things, and places a negative filter on the way you think.

If this happens to you, the first step is to remind yourself how close is the relationship between thoughts and feelings. Think about a time when you felt different, more positive and happy and scan your memory for specific examples of how you thought about things then. You will need to see if you can amplify the scanner, and focus it clearly, as such examples can become nearly invisible when a low mood spreads a confusing, obscuring haze over everything.

It's worth remembering...

Feeling that something is true does not make it true.

Although feeling low about yourself does make it difficult at first to see things another way, focus hard on the specifics of exactly what happened, and disentangle the facts from your feelings about the facts.

Make a list here of some of the times when you weren't anxious or shy and a social occasion went well for you. Look at this list at other times when you're feeling unhappy or depressed about a recent social event.

My social successes:

_____

_____

_____

_____

_____

_____

Look back to page 3 of Part One. Reminding yourself of your strengths, qualities and talents may help you. Remembering social events that went well may also help you.

How to make it easier for yourself

Most people who have suffered from social anxiety or shyness try hard to overcome their difficulties. Like them, you probably do whatever you can – and often people's ideas are good ones.

- You may try to keep going, and not to run away from things.

- You may try to 'say something to yourself to make you feel better' – which is a fairly good description of the general aim of cognitive therapy.

- You may try not to dwell on the problem and on the uncomfortable sensations that it produces.

- You may try to relax and to keep things in perspective, and to build your life as best you can.

So it is not for want of trying that the problem of social anxiety persists. Targeting these efforts more effectively and more efficiently, so that you succeed in breaking the vicious cycles that otherwise keep social anxiety going, is highly likely to be more helpful. But it may be difficult at first. Doing new things in new ways can be alarming and feel risky. Helping yourself takes courage and it takes persistence.

If you knew someone else who was undertaking such a task, how would you set about helping them? What would they require from you? Three important contributions to their efforts would be:

1 Compassion

2 Understanding

3 Encouragement.

Unfortunately it seems to be far easier to see how to give these things to someone else than to yourself. Most people make themselves exceptions to the rule when it comes to 'self-improvement', or 'self-help'. Instead they go in for self-blame, criticism and name calling. We say things like, 'It was all my fault', 'I'm clumsy and awkward', 'Wimp', 'Coward'. These are obvious examples of negative and unhelpful ways of thinking, and shy or anxious people can be far more creative than this when putting themselves down.

It would be easier to make effective changes if you became more compassionate with yourself. Spend some time working out how to understand your own particular version of social anxiety and what keeps it going. This is much more likely to help and encourage you in your effort to change. Although this may sound obvious – or trivial or patronizing – it is a very important point. It is far too easy to ignore the damaging effect of saying such negative and harsh things to yourself.

Let's now summarize the main ideas in this section and look at some more ideas about how to put them together. In this way you'll be able to use them effectively to change the way you feel, and to help you when you start to do things differently.

Putting the steps together

The two steps for changing thinking patterns are:

1 Learning how to identify what is in your mind

2 Learning how to re-examine the ways you think.

Putting these two steps together helps you to get better at finding the ways of thinking that make you feel better, and it also helps you think about how to put the new ways of thinking into effect: how to start changing your behaviour as well as your thinking. Changing behaviour is the topic of Section 4. Here we will concentrate on combining the steps for changing patterns of thinking.

The way to do this is shown in the thought record overleaf, and blank copies of the complete thought record can be found at the back of this book.

Writing about changes in feelings

You will notice that there are extra columns in the complete thought record that did not appear in the two earlier versions of it on pages 64 and 65. The first of these, 'Change in feelings', is for noting down how working on your thoughts changed the way you felt: all of the options are available, from making you feel much worse (–10), through no change at all (0), to making you feel much better (+10).

As you will see from the examples, some new ways of thinking have less effect than others. Some, like the last one shown here, may still give you some ideas about what to do even if they do not, at the time, make you feel any better. Remember, you are looking for new ways of thinking that make you feel better and that help you to do the things that you want to do. It may take some practice before you can bring them to mind when you need them.

Complete thought record

Situation (be specific)	Upsetting thoughts (keep the different thoughts separate)	Possible alternatives (there may be more than one)	Change in feelings (−10 to +10)	Action plan (what would you like to do differently?)
Talking to C. at a party. Getting stuck.	I've got nothing to contribute.	Not 'nothing', just rather little. I have, but I can't get it out.	A bit better: probably +2 or 3	Think how to start conversations. Listen to how other people do it
	He must think I'm hopeless.	I don't know what he is thinking. There are two of us here. It could be partly him.		Move away when I get stuck, and try talking to someone else.
Picking up my drink from the table, in the pub with sports team; hands shaking.	They will notice the shaking. It gives me away.	OK, they might notice. But shaking is no big deal. Anyone might do it sometimes.	A lot better in theory. If I could really believe this I would feel +8. In fact it's about +6.	Try to stop bothering about the shaking, and do things anyway. Start talking to people more, instead of noticing how I feel.
	They will see through me, and discover how inadequate I am.	They seem to need me on the team, so I can't be totally inadequate.		
Dreading going to work. Hoping no one will ask what I did at the weekend.	I could call in sick.	That would only make me feel worse: and ashamed of myself.	Still dread going, but know I will feel better if I do than if I don't.	I could ask people what they did, and see if it gives me more ideas. I need to plan something, whether or not there's someone to do it with.
	I could invent something to tell them.	Yes, but it wouldn't be true and they might catch me out.		
	Everyone else but me has a busy social life.	Maybe. But maybe not too. I don't really know – yet.	Probably still feel just as anxious: no change = 0.	

Action plan

The second new column is headed 'Action plan'. This is where you should write down what you would like to do differently. The point of this column is to remind you that you will gain most if you are able to put the new ways of thinking into effect to change your behaviour as well as your thinking. Section 4 explains more about how to do this. For now you should think about what you would like to be able to do differently, so that you can then work towards this.

You can use any of the ideas in this book to start you thinking about what kind of action plan you would like to be able to make for yourself. The examples in the completed record shown on the previous page have been written to illustrate how to use this worksheet, and should make the whole process clear. But remember, if you have difficulty with it, you can adapt it to suit your needs better.

Be honest

It is important to be honest with yourself when you fill in these worksheets. This is the case even if facing up to the difficulties that you have and to negative thoughts makes you feel worse at first – or makes you feel embarrassed. As you get better at finding alternatives, you will be able to use the method to change the way you feel, and to devise the action plan that you want.

Write it down

It is also important to do this exercise on paper. Thinking things through in your head is far more difficult than it might seem. It is easy to skim over difficulties or to formulate rather vague alternatives and plans if they do not have to be written down.

As the method becomes familiar to you, writing things down will no longer be necessary. You'll be able to do more of it in your head, in the situations that actually provoke your anxiety. But writing things down is important when you begin. As Sally, the shy woman we met earlier, said when she tried this, there is a risk at first of being suddenly carried away on a mounting rollercoaster of anxiety, and of getting in such a flap that you can no longer think rationally or clearly. However, what she discovered was that if she found a way of taking a break and calming down, then she could 'take stock and get a grip', and rational thought could return. She also reminded herself that she was trying to change patterns of thinking that had been there for years – and no one had said it would be easy. This kind of work does get easier with practice. And when these methods for changing patterns of thinking are combined with those we look at in the following sections on reducing self-consciousness, changing patterns of behaviour and building confidence, then you are well on the way to overcoming social anxiety.

Complete thought record

Situation	Upsetting thoughts	Possible alternatives	Change in feelings (−10 to +10)	Action plan

Making flashcards, to help you remember new patterns of thinking

Old patterns of thinking are like bad habits, and tend to come back again and again. It is only too easy to slip into your favourite biased ways of thinking (see pages 53–57). One way of helping yourself to break these old habits is to make flashcards that help you to develop new habits. Flashcards are small reminders of new ways of thinking that you can carry around with you. Cards are useful because they last longer than bits of paper, and they can be put in your pocket or wallet and kept to hand easily.

So get yourself a card, and on one side of it write one of your typical upsetting thoughts, such as:

- 'Everyone can see how nervous I am'

- 'I always make a fool of myself'

- 'They think I'm not worth having around'

or a question about your favourite bias:

- 'Am I mind-reading again?'

On the other side write down the alternative ways of thinking that you think are helpful. For example:

- 'I feel more nervous than I look'

- 'I have handled things okay many times before'

- 'I know I have something worthwhile to contribute'.

Use the back of the card to summarize the work you have done, and to remind yourself of other ways of thinking, and of things that have happened that go against your old patterns of thinking.

Carry the card with you at all times. Then you can use it whenever you need:

- When going out to do something difficult

- As you arrive somewhere and before you go in to do whatever you have come to do

- After you leave and before the undermining post mortem begins

- To give yourself a much-needed boost if your confidence feels as if it is flagging.

Write some of your key ideas, positive thoughts or reminders about your anxious style of thinking here. Then copy them on to a card.

Summary

1 Thoughts affect how you feel, and feelings affect how you think. Changing the way you think will help you to feel better. There are many different kinds of thoughts, many of which most people never have to express in words.

2 The first step is to identify the ways you think.

3 Some patterns of thinking reflect biases. Biased ways of thinking are unlikely to be right. Many of us have 'favourite' biases, and if you know what they are it will be easier to work against them.

4 The second step is to look for alternative ways of thinking.

5 Good alternatives can usually be expressed in moderate or balanced terms.

6 Doubting yourself and saying 'Yes, but ...' makes finding alternatives difficult.

7 It is easier to find alternatives if you use the kind of compassionate, understanding and encouraging approach that you would adopt if you were helping someone else.

8 Completing thought records is extremely helpful. Although the exercises in this chapter can be done in your head, they will be much more effective and much more useful to you in the long run if you also practise doing them on paper.

9 Copies of the three thought records used in this section can be found at the back of this book.

10 Summarize the work you do on a flashcard, and use it as a reminder of new and more helpful ways of thinking.

SECTION 4: Doing Things Differently

This section will help you to understand how to start changing the way you behave:

- How to perform mini-experiments in doing things differently

- How to change your safety behaviours

- How to stop avoiding things

- How to keep a record of your experiments

- Why you don't have to learn how to behave 'correctly'

- How to start taking risks

- How to handle setbacks and feeling anxious.

Before you start work on this section, remember that thoughts, feelings and behaviour are closely linked. That is why the previous section on changing the way you think is so important. If you think that you do not fit in well with the people around you, then you may feel dispirited, and behave in ways that reduce the amount of contact you have with them. So it is important to both think differently and act differently. The two together will help you feel less anxious and happier.

New ways of doing things

In this section we will look at experimenting with new ways of doing things such as:

- Being more outgoing

- Asking more questions

- Making the effort to meet new people.

Acting in new ways provides a direct test of what you think about social situations. It challenges anxious predictions you may have about what will happen such as:

- 'I shall feel dreadful the whole time'

- 'I won't be able to get my point across. I will get muddled and confused'.

Thoughts like these make you want to protect yourself and keep yourself safe. But avoiding things or holding yourself back means that you never know if your predictions are right. Taking the risk of doing things differently can tell you whether the predictions you were making were right or wrong. You might have been upsetting yourself for no good reason.

Most people with social anxiety want to protect themselves from the embarrassments and humiliations that they fear. But if you try to keep yourself safe from disaster, and avoid doing things that make you feel at risk, your life becomes restricted.

Often the way you are thinking and feeling makes keeping safe seem like the only sensible option. Safety behaviours and avoidance are understandable reactions to feeling anxious, but in the long run they maintain the difficulty rather than resolve it. Dealing with thoughts is a beginning, but changing your behaviour is essential if you are going to overcome social anxiety.

What would changing your behaviour mean?

It is important to recognize the ways in which being socially anxious or shy affect your behaviour. When you do this you'll gain the most from this section. Let's look at some key questions to help you really focus in on the way you behave now and how you'd like to change. We'll see how Joe, a 28-year-old man with social anxiety, answered these questions and then we want you to answer them for yourself.

The four key questions

1   What would you like to do?

Think of something you would like to do but haven't done because of being socially anxious. Some examples may help you start thinking along the right lines:

- Make the first move towards getting to know someone better

- Ask someone you do not know well to do something with you

- Look for a new job

- Disagree with someone in authority

- Make requests such as asking someone to help you out, or turn their music down, or give you the pay rise you deserve

- Invite people into your home

- Accept the offer of further training or a position with more responsibility or a promotion

- Take advantage of an opportunity to stretch yourself and acquire a new skill.

Joe wrote:

I would like to be more outgoing with my work colleague, Colette.

Write down here what you would like to do if you felt less anxious:

_____

_____

_____

_____

2 What would happen if you did what you would like to do?

Now ask yourself what gets in the way of doing things that you would like to do, and prevents you realizing your potential.

You might well answer: 'my social anxiety'. But think about this question more deeply and ask yourself what these situations mean to you. Do you, for instance, see them as sources of potential embarrassment and humiliation that make them seem too risky to attempt?

It is as if trying to do these things would put too much at stake. Something might go wrong. The dangers and threats are inhibiting and hold you back. The meaning that they have for you interferes with the way you would otherwise behave.

Write down here what you think would go wrong if you did do the things you would like to do.

Joe wrote:

I might make some stupid joke that wasn't funny. Colette would think I was an idiot.

Your answer:

_____

_____

_____

3   What would happen if your prediction was wrong?

When something seems threatening you think about how to protect yourself. There are two main ways of doing this:

1   Keeping yourself safe

2   Avoiding things.

Giving up safety behaviours and avoidance helps you to find out whether these threats are truly serious or not. If your prediction is wrong the threat will diminish for you as you face the things that you fear. In this way you are continuing the process of change that you began by working on your thoughts.

4   If your prediction was wrong, and things consistently turned out better than you feared they might, what would it mean to you? What would it mean about you?

Joe wrote:

If I was more outgoing and expressed my personality Colette would get to know me better. We might actually get closer and become real friends. It would mean that I would be less lonely. It would mean that I could be myself and people would accept me for who I am.

Write down your answer here.

_____

_____

_____

_____

Thinking about what you've done

The idea of these questions is to make you **think** about what you would be able to do if you were not so anxious or shy, and about what it would mean if you could. When you follow through the ideas below and start to change what you do, we want you to also follow through these changes by **thinking** about their implications.

Changing your behaviour and doing things that you find difficult is important. But it is most effective if you stop and think about what you have done afterwards. Let's look more closely at why this is so crucial.

How to make lasting changes

Many people who are socially anxious go on doing things that they fear, even when they feel terrible. They go to places where they will meet new people, or eat in other people's houses, or go to work social events. But they find that doing the things that they fear has no lasting effect. They want to realize their potential and to be themselves. And they think, correctly, that not doing these things is likely to make them worse. But often their courage is not rewarded, as the problem persists despite it.

Why does this happen? One reason is that the courageous action, or change in behaviour on its own, has no real meaning for you. It does not change your expectations and predictions about what might happen next time unless you work on these too. You can always dismiss the occasional success as a lucky break, or assume that other people rather than you were responsible for its successful aspects.

Faithfully follow all four of the steps described below for dealing with safety behaviours and avoidance. Then think about the changes you are making as you go along. This will help you get lasting results. You will be able to test out your predictions as you go, and really notice and be aware of your changes. Eventually this will give new meaning to your interactions with other people – and indeed to the times when these interactions do not go according to plan.

Ways of doing things differently: mini-experiments

No special skills are needed to change your behaviour. It is not as if you have to learn a whole new language. It's more like finding a way of releasing you from what holds you back so that you can be yourself and feel more comfortable with that.

The two main ways of behaving differently are:

1 Giving up safety behaviours

2 Facing things rather than avoiding them.

The main method that helps you decide how to do things differently is to carry out mini-experiments. To do this all you need to be able to do is to be curious about what happens when you do things differently. There are four main steps you need to follow in a mini experiment. They apply to both safety behaviours and avoidance. Let's look at them now in terms of changing safety behaviours.

Changing safety behaviours

As we've seen earlier, one of the difficulties about social situations is that you cannot control other people. At any moment they may do something that you find threatening, like ask your opinion, or introduce you to the person you feel least able to talk to, or move away while you are talking to them. Safety behaviours are things that you do to protect yourself from such threats. We looked at them earlier in Part One, Section 7, page 91.

The problem with safety behaviours

There are three main problems with safety behaviours.

1   *Decreasing your confidence*

Safety behaviours decrease your confidence in the long run because they leave you with the message that you need protection: that you would be unsafe without it.

For example, Joe, whom we met earlier, practised a safety behaviour of not making eye contact with people he didn't know well. His social anxiety made him tongue-tied and he felt that if he looked someone in the eye that might make them ask him a question. In this way his safety behaviour prevented him from behaving in a more socially confident way.

2   *Preventing you from learning*

Using safety behaviours also has the effect of suggesting that they worked: that they succeeded in preventing the threat occurring, or the disaster happening.

So when Joe looked away when talking to other people he effectively moved out of the conversation, leaving other people to take it up. No one seemed to realize how blank he felt as the conversation went on. It left him out of the conversation loop but it didn't make him the focus of a social awkwardness, or provoke an embarrassing silence. He felt safer but he was also preventing himself from having any interactions that might have helped him change and grow. Safety behaviours, like letting your hair fall in front of your face, or smoking so as to have something to do with your hands, keep the problem going as they prevent you learning that the disasters you fear are more imagined than real.

3 *Making the situation worse*

Safety behaviours can also make the situation worse, especially when they become noticeable, or if they provoke a reaction from others.

For example, trying not to draw attention to yourself by speaking quietly may mean that someone asks you to repeat what you have just said. You have to say it again more loudly, with everyone listening. In the same way, saying nothing personal about yourself, so that you keep the 'real you' hidden, can make people curious about you – especially if they want to be friendly – so they start asking probing questions.

What are your safety behaviours?

Everyone invents their own safety behaviours, so only you know exactly what you do. Some common examples include:

- Looking down so no one can catch your eye

- Wearing light clothing in case you get hot and sweaty

- Leaving the room immediately the meeting or event is over so that you do not have to get involved in 'small talk'

- Trying to be especially careful about what you say, or to make sure that it makes sense

- Keeping an eye on possible escape routes when you feel uncomfortable, and arming yourself ahead of time with excuses for getting away

- Trying not to attract unwanted attention.

Steps towards giving up safety behaviours

There are four steps to go through, and all four together make up a mini-experiment.

1 Become aware of what you do to protect yourself

2 Identifying what you predict would happen if you did not do it. This specifies the danger from which the safety behaviour would protect you

3 Find out what happens if you give up the safety behaviour

4 Draw conclusions from what you have done.

Let's now look at each of these steps in more detail.

Step 1: Identifying what you do

In order to solve the problem of safety behaviours you need first to become aware of them. This is not so easy as it might seem. Some of them may be so much of a habit that you no longer notice them. There may be things that only you know you are doing, like rehearsing in advance what you want to say, or ones that others can see, like wearing the 'right' sorts of clothes. There are also likely to be things that you do not do such as talking about yourself and your feelings, or telling a story or a joke.

Think about a recent situation that you found difficult. Now ask yourself what you did to ensure that you did not feel too vulnerable or exposed. You might also find it useful to think about what would have made the situation worse for you, like having to talk without notes, or not being able to have a drink before you went out. Using 'props' is a common way of keeping safe.

Other people could also form part of your safety behaviours. Do some people provide a 'reassuring presence' for you, so that just having them around makes you feel better? Do you use them as part of your safety system?

Answer these key questions to help you identify your safety behaviours

1 What do you do to prevent bad things happening?

_____

_____

_____

_____

_____

2 How do you protect yourself from the social embarrassments that you fear?

_____

_____

_____

_____

_____

3 If you feel suddenly at risk, what is the first thing you do?

_____

_____

_____

_____

_____

4 What do you do to prevent other people noticing your symptoms?

_____

_____

_____

_____

_____

5 What do you do to ensure that you do not do anything wrong?

_____

_____

_____

_____

_____

6 What do you do to hide your problem or to stop it showing?

_____

_____

_____

_____

_____

Now summarize your safety behaviours as a list in the space below. You can keep adding to this as you think of more safety behaviours.

My safety behaviours:

_____

_____

_____

_____

_____

Step 2: Making a prediction

Step 2 involves thinking about what would happen if you gave up your safety behaviours, and stopped trying to protect yourself. Think about specific times and events when you have felt bad. Pick a particular one that you can remember clearly. Or start by thinking about something that might happen quite soon, and ask yourself what you fear might happen to you.

There are many questions you could ask yourself at this stage, for example:

- What are you predicting will happen?

- What is it that you fear will go wrong for you?

- What would happen if you did not protect yourself?

But the most important **key question** to answer is this one:

What is the worst thing that could happen to you?

Make sure that you let yourself 'look into the abyss' and try to put into words the catastrophe that you predict will happen. Write it down in the space opposite, to make sure that you know exactly what it is.

Sometimes your worst fear, on inspection, sounds not too bad when brought out into the open. Sometimes it sounds so extreme that you can immediately see that it is not likely to be correct – like thinking that everyone will openly point at you, or laugh at you.

Other predictions have more reality behind them. Louise, who let her hair fall in front of her face to hide her blushes, feared that people would ridicule her – as indeed her school friends once had – if they saw her hot, red face glowing like a beacon when someone spoke to her. Bill, who kept trying to tell jokes at work, feared that he would be rejected and become totally isolated if he did not join in the general banter.

My prediction:

_____

_____

_____

_____

_____

Making a prediction testable

Now that you've got your worst nightmare out in the open, let's look at what you wrote more closely. Think about how you've worded your prediction. Is it going to be testable in a real life situation?

Predictions about yourself are perhaps the easiest to test. For example you could test the following ideas easily:

- 'I'll shake, and spill my drink.'

- 'My anxiety will get out of control.'

Predictions about other people need to be specific if they are going to be testable. You might predict that other people will stare at you, or that they will ignore you. These predictions about how other people will behave can be tested. But no experiments are likely to reveal exactly what other people think of you. Predictions about other people's thoughts and attitudes are very hard to test.

In order to test a prediction about being rejected and becoming totally isolated, for example, you would first have to work out how you would know if this was happening. You would have to decide on the signs that would tell you you were being rejected. And you'd have to be sure that you were not using very vague and general behaviour, like someone turning away from you, or yawning, as signs of rejection. These things could happen for many other reasons. The person might have suddenly heard their name called or be tired, for example. The signs leave too much room for you to give your own personal and anxiety-driven meaning to them.

In this case it would be better to test the specific prediction that you will feel rejected, or that other people will not start conversations with you, or that they will not respond to your comments, look you in the eye, or ask you to join them and so on.

When people predict other people's reactions to them, for example predicting that they will not take them seriously, it is especially difficult to make the prediction testable. How would you know whether people took you seriously? How would anyone know? You could decide what would count as **not** being taken seriously, and define specific criteria for that, like never listening to what you say, or always ignoring your opinion. But definitions that use 'extremist' words, like 'never' and 'always' are only rarely likely to be true (see page 68).

The point here is that sometimes the attempt to look for specific predictions itself reveals that the prediction is so general – or so **over-general** – that it is most unlikely to be correct. It will be most helpful if you make specific predictions that seem realistic to you. Then testing them out will tell you something you did not already know.

With this in mind, try rewriting your prediction so that it really is testable.

_____

_____

_____

_____

_____

Step 3: Find out what happens if you give up using your safety behaviours

This is the point at which you have to think about how to change your behaviour: about the kind of mini-experiment you will carry out.

Think first of a situation in which you would like things to be different, such as using the telephone when other people are listening, or starting a conversation with someone. Write it down here.

_____

_____

_____

_____

_____

Now think about what you will do differently. Be quite specific about it. You should choose one of the safety behaviours on your list and create an experiment for yourself, to test out what happens if you go into this situation 'unprotected'. Here are some experiments you could try:

- Look people in the eye when you talk to them instead of avoiding eye contact

- Say what you think instead of just agreeing with them

- Relax your grip on the telephone or the pencil or the coffee mug instead of tensing yourself up in an effort to control the shaking.

Louise, who tried to hide her blushes, carried out the experiment of tying back her hair and holding her head up straight, in full view of everyone around her. Bill, who kept trying to tell jokes, tried keeping quiet until he had something to say instead.

The aim is to find out if the danger you fear is real. In order to do this you need to drop your armour and see if the disaster you fear comes to pass.

Write down what you will do differently here.

_____

_____

_____

_____

_____

_____

Taking action is the hardest step, and the one that feels most risky at first. But it is worth doing because it starts the process of building up your confidence. If you feel anxious the first time you do something differently, try again and see if by degrees your anxiety starts to die down.

A reminder: there is no fixed, rigid and right way of doing things socially; there are many ways. Your way, once you have learned to relax and to be yourself, will be just as good as the next person's.

Trying to keep yourself safe tends to make you more tense and inflexible than you otherwise would be. Even though it feels alarming at first, giving up your safety behaviours, once you have got used to doing without them, allows you to adapt as the situation unfolds, and frees you up to interact in new and more natural ways.

Step 4: Evaluate what happens

Think about what actually happened when you behaved differently. Make sure that you are sticking with the facts and not jumping to conclusions about what other people thought, or assuming that because you felt anxious you did something stupid or revealed your basic weaknesses.

Ask yourself: Did the prediction come true? Were you right? Or were you misled by your anxiety? Were you seeing things in an alarming light because of your fear rather than the facts? Are you sure that your observations fit with the facts rather than with they way you felt about the facts? Write down what happened here.

_____

_____

_____

_____

_____

On page 97 you will find a worksheet for recording your mini experiments in changing your safety behaviours. There are extra blank copies at the back of the book. We have completed a worksheet on page 96 as a guide to help you fill in yours. It takes a surprising amount of practice to evaluate your mini experiments accurately and well. Completing the worksheet will help you to make the most of the experiments that you do.

What if the worst thing happens?

Dropping safety behaviours will feel risky. It will take courage, because it always seems possible that the thing you fear most will really happen. There are two answers to this problem.

1   The thing that you most fear very rarely does happen.

Indeed, what you fear is more likely to happen if you keep using the safety behaviour than if you give it up. For example, Louise, who kept trying to hide her blushes was actually drawing attention to herself when she tried to hide. She attracted the attention she was trying to avoid, and this made her more likely to blush. When she stopped trying to hide, and let the blushes come and go as they pleased, she realized that other people took their cue from her. They too paid little attention to the blushes, and continued to interact with her in a perfectly normal way.

And Bill, who stopped trying to tell jokes and keep up the banter with his colleagues at work, quickly realized that the tense and nervous jokes he usually contributed had mostly fallen flat. They were more likely to invite the ridicule that he feared than allowing himself to be the quiet person that he really was.

2 If the thing that you fear happens, it may not actually be a disaster

Imagine you have kept yourself safe by never letting anyone know what you feel, and by not saying what you really think. Then you decide to take your courage in both hands, and to disclose something important about yourself to someone you respect. The result is they seem to dismiss you and your feelings, or they seem bored and uninterested. Ask yourself:

- How would you know what they thought?

- And what they felt?

- Or what their reactions meant?

- Could they have misunderstood what you said?

- Or were they being insensitive because they did not realize how important it was for you?

The fact is that often other people do not respond in the ways that you hope they will, but there are many reasons for this. Socially anxious people tend to take such happenings personally, and to mind read. Remember, other people's unhelpful or insensitive reactions do not make you less acceptable as a person, or make your feelings less important and meaningful.

Facing the fears by stopping avoiding things

Avoidance is not doing something because it makes you fearful or anxious. We first looked at avoidance in Part One, Section 2, page 14. It is one of the more extreme versions of keeping safe. There are many kinds of avoidance, and some of them are easier to recognize than others. Examples of obvious types of avoidance include:

- Not going to places where you know you will meet people

- Not using the telephone

Thought record for changing behaviours

Specific situation (Think of a situation in which you use a safety behaviour)	Prediction (What will happen if you do not keep yourself safe? How will you know if it happens?)	Experiment (How will you find out? What will you do differently?)	What actually happened? (What did you observe? Stick to the facts.)	Conclusions (What does this mean?)
Hiding my face when someone in the office asks me a question	I will blush and go bright red. They will look away, and stop talking to me.	I will stop hiding myself, stay in full view, and let them see what happens.	I did go red. But I did not hide, and the conversation just went on.	That going red is not as disastrous as I feared. That I don't need to hide.
A pause in the conversation when I start talking nonsense just to fill in the gap	The silence will go on, and no one will speak. My anxiety will get out of control, and become visible to everyone.	I will try saying nothing, and waiting for someone else to break the silence.	I did feel highly anxious, but everyone else just went on talking when they were ready.	I'm not the only one responsible for keeping things going.
Going out at a time when I am unlikely to meet, or have to talk to, people I know	People will approach me, and say something that I should answer. I will feel nervous, and say something stupid.	I will go out at busier times, answer if someone speaks to me, and not cross the street to avoid anyone.	I felt very nervous, but I answered someone who said 'Good morning'. OK. I passed someone I knew, but they said nothing.	I suppose I could get used to it. People don't seem to be that interested in talking anyway, in those circumstances.

Thought record for changing behaviours

Specific situation (Think of a situation in which you use a safety behaviour)	Prediction (What will happen if you do not keep yourself safe? How will you know if it happens?)	Experiment (How will you find out? What will you do differently?)	What actually happened? (What did you observe? Stick to the facts.)	Conclusions (What does this mean?)

- Not eating in public or asking questions

- Not speaking to strangers

- Not asking someone out for a date

- Refusing invitations.

And there are many others.

More subtle types of avoidance are so familiar, and so much part and parcel of the way people behave when they are socially anxious, that often they are not even aware of doing them. They include not starting conversations or not initiating contact with people; not accepting a challenge; or never doing things on your own.

Some people become very good at skimming the surface of social situations, and might make a habit of arriving at them late and leaving early. At a party you could still subtly avoid talking to people by helping with the food and drink, or with the clearing up, and find a way of only half paying attention to other people.

Bob, who had severe social phobia, described this as being 'both there and not there', and for him it happened whenever he was with a group of people who were talking among themselves. He wanted to be part of the conversation, and to feel that he belonged to the group and was accepted by them. But he still disengaged himself, and felt detached for much of the time. Perhaps you know what he meant.

Experiments for facing things rather than avoiding them

The same four steps we used for giving up safety behaviours can also be used to plan how to face rather than avoid the things that you find difficult:

1 Identify what you avoid.

2 Make a prediction. Link your avoidance with what you think would happen if you stopped avoiding.

3 Do something differently: in this case, face the fear rather than avoid it.

4 Evaluate what happens. Think about what happened, as objectively as you can. Then work out whether your thoughts about what might happen were right.

Step 1: Identify what you avoid

The first step sounds relatively easy, and often it is. However, when thinking about precisely what you avoid, remember that you are probably the only person who knows exactly what that is, and how you manage to avoid it. Try to notice when you feel like avoiding something, and when you get that sense of wanting to withdraw or hide yourself away that leads to avoidance. A good test of whether you are avoiding something or not is to ask: 'If I were confident, would I do it?'

Write down here some of the things you avoid.

_____

_____

_____

_____

_____

Step 2: Predict what would happen

The second step involves asking yourself what you predict, or expect might happen if you did the thing you are avoiding. In this way you'll be able to identify how the way you think links up with your avoidance.

What is your worst fear? Do you have any memories or images about similar situations that explain why they seem to you to be so alarming? The key questions for identifying thoughts may be useful here; see Section 3, page 47.

Write down your prediction or fear here.

_____

_____

_____

_____

_____

Step 3: Face your fear

The third step, facing the fear rather than avoiding it, is always the hardest. Often it helps to build your confidence up by doing easier things before you move on to harder ones.

You could start by greeting people when you meet them and build up to full-length conversations. Or you could start by listening to others and watching what they do, and build up to asking someone out for a date. Or you could involve yourself in helpful activities in your local neighbourhood, or join an evening class, as a step on the way to making more personal relationships and better friendships. Your aim should be to be able to do the thing that you are avoiding.

Write down here ways in which you could face your fear.

_____

_____

_____

_____

_____

Step 4: Assessing what happened

The fourth step has two parts:

1 Observing what actually happened

2 Working out how this fits with what you originally thought.

It is only too easy to dismiss or to discount the things that happen as a result of carrying out experiments, especially if nothing in particular goes wrong. If you managed to do something new for you, like make an appointment to get your hair cut, then it is easy to think of this as the kind of normal activity that should present you with no particular problems.

This is why it is so important to identify your predictions about what might happen before you go ahead and do something that you might not otherwise do. Doing it this way allows you to find out whether your predictions are confirmed or not.

For example, you might expect to feel embarrassed and humiliated by having to watch yourself in the mirror while having your hair cut, or predict that the person cutting your hair will make a personal remark about you, or ask you personal questions. If you know exactly what you expect to happen, you can find out whether your expectations are confirmed or were wrong.

In this way, doing things differently can help to change the way you think as well as to change what you do. Next time your expectations and predictions, based on your new findings, should be different.

Write down here what actually happened in your first experiment. How does it compare with your prediction?

_____

_____

_____

_____

_____

Keeping records of your experiments

Keep a written record of the risks that you take, and of what happens at the time, using the worksheet on page 102. There are extra copies at the back of the book. If you don't do this you will not know how you are getting on. It is surprising how easy it is to forget, especially when a success for you (for example, using the telephone when people can hear what you say) may very normal for someone else. A written record allows you to see clearly what you are changing, and it helps you plan what to do next.

Other kinds of experiment

Using experiments to guide you when you decide to do something differently is a way of making the most of everything that you do. It helps to ensure that the changes in how you think, feel and act fit together. When this happens your confidence will grow more quickly. For this reason it is worth being as creative and imaginative as you can when thinking up experiments to change your behaviour.

We have focused here on how to change safety behaviours and how to face things instead of avoiding them, but there are also other kinds of experiments you could do. For example, you could go to some places as an observer, instead of a participant, and notice what other people do, and whether any of them show signs of being anxious or shy.

Or you could experiment with the elements of social interaction, the things that keep social communication going. These include:

- Listening to other people

- Looking at them

Thought record for facing fears

Specific situation (Think of a situation that you avoid)	Prediction (What will happen if you do not avoid this?)	Experiment (How will you face your fear? What will you do?)	What actually happened? (What did you observe? Stick to the facts)	Conclusions (What does this mean?)

- Working out what they feel about what they are saying

- Asking questions when you want to find out about others

- Saying what you think

- Expressing your feelings.

These all help people to join in with others, and give them a better sense of belonging rather than feeling like an outsider. Experiment with doing them more and with doing them less than usual, to find out what effect this has.

Another experiment that can be useful is intentionally to make your symptoms worse. This is particularly helpful for people who fear that their symptoms will be noticed – and think that it matters when they are. So you could make yourself shake visibly, or stumble over your words when saying something, or repeat yourself on purpose, and then observe what happens. Identify your prediction first: the catastrophe that you fear. Then use your observation to find out whether your prediction was right.

This is very hard to do for people who believe that there is a right – and therefore a wrong – way of doing things, and that their way is bound to be wrong. But for them, the experiment is also especially helpful.

Should you be trying to learn how to do things right?

In a way shyness and social anxiety are all about what you do: about what you fear you might do, or might not do. The fear is that you will act in a way that will be humiliating or embarrassing, or **do something** that reveals your symptoms of anxiety. You think you will **behave** in a way that is unacceptable, or **do** something wrong – knock something over, or blurt out something personal at an inappropriate moment.

The fear of showing yourself up by the way you act prevents you behaving naturally (and unselfconsciously). But focusing on changing behaviours is not about learning how to 'do things right'. Nor is it about learning how to behave so that 'bad' things do not happen to you. Nothing you can do will guarantee protection from the occasional rejection, or moment when you feel embarrassed and painfully conspicuous.

Everyone has times when they cannot think of anything of any interest to say to anyone; when they are undeniably boring. Social awkwardnesses will continue to plague us all, but the meaning of them can change.

- Social problems can come to feel less dangerous and threatening

- They can stop holding you back from being yourself

- They can have less devastating implications for your sense of adequacy or acceptability.

They will become more like making a trivial mistake such as leaving your umbrella behind or running out of toothpaste.

Why experiments work

Changing behaviours has a powerful effect partly because it allows you to do the things that you want to do, and also because it can help to change meanings. Carrying out experiments such as the ones we've looked at in this section allows you to re-evaluate social threats and dangers so that they come to have a different meaning for you. They make it possible to find out whether your more anxious predictions and expectations, for example about how you might embarrass or humiliate yourself, are correct.

Changing what you do is another way of finding out whether taking another viewpoint, or adopting another standpoint, helps you to feel more confident when interacting with others. So changing your behaviour also helps you to realize your potential and to be yourself.

Social conventions

Some people think that in order to get better they should learn how to behave correctly, as if there were a right way of doing things. There are some situations in which the conventional ways of doing things are rather like rules, and then it can certainly feel more comfortable to know what the rules are. For example, it's useful to know how to:

- Order a meal at a restaurant

- Make an appointment to see the doctor

- Do what is expected of you as a member of a sports club or church or evening class or committee.

Learning the rules in such situations is a bit like learning a 'script'– the script is useful because it tells you how to behave. But remember, rule books are not written with flexibility in mind. Sometimes it is not possible to use the usual script even though you would like to, for example when someone starts a personal conversation with you at work, or if you meet your doctor in the supermarket.

Rules and scripts are helpful, but they can also be limiting. Let's look at Jenny's story to get a better understanding of the problem.

CASE STUDY: Jenny

Jenny was an efficient and busy hotel receptionist. Although she had suffered from social anxiety most of her life, she had very little difficulty carrying out her job. She had been well trained, and had been told exactly how to handle the various types of problems that arose in her work, including dealing with complaints and rudeness from guests. She had been able to rehearse and practise all the skills that she needed on the job, and applying these skills was merely a matter of following the rules. There was nothing personal about it. Indeed, she could do the job regardless of how she was feeling at the time, as it had become rather like switching into automatic, and putting on her professional mask.

But although Jenny knew her 'script' well, without it she felt, literally, 'unmasked'. In more personal situations, when there were no rules to guide her, she felt at sea and at risk. She was deeply embarrassed by not being able to think what to say to a colleague whom she met when out for a walk at the weekend. Her first attempts to overcome the problem involved looking for the rules of the game: hunting for a 'script' that would help her out. But she'd never been trained for this type of situation. She didn't have any rules to fall back on. In the end she muttered an excuse about having to get home and left as fast as she could. When she got home she felt disappointed and angry with herself for not being able to do something so ordinary.

Jenny's story shows us that more personal, and especially more intimate, relationships develop their own conventions. This means that you may not always know exactly what to do ahead of time. Instead you have to learn to do what feels right, and to respond flexibly to the demands of the situation as it develops without being self-conscious. This is much easier if you can focus comfortably on other people, as you learned to do in Section 2, pages 33-38.

This section will help you to develop the confidence to adapt the way you behave to the situation that you find yourself in. The emphasis is on thinking about how to realize your potential rather than looking for rules or conventions. In their own way these can limit your ability to express yourself in the way that feels right to you.

You don't need any special skills to be able to do this. It comes without teaching, and is more a matter of feeling able to be yourself, and finding the ways of doing so that work for you rather than against you. Being able to pay attention to others and to respond to their part in the interaction also helps you to develop the flexibility to learn as you go. There are some special skills that it can be helpful to learn such as assertiveness and relaxation techniques. We look at these in Part Three. You already have all the skills that you need for using the ideas in this section, although it is certainly possible that when you are feeling anxious it may be harder to use them.

Taking risks and making mistakes

Changing behaviours involves taking risks. One of the things that holds people back is the fear of making mistakes. This will seem more risky if you think that mistakes matter: if you think that the mistakes you make will make others think badly of you, or draw attention to you (however temporarily).

But everyone makes mistakes, most of which are invisible to anyone but themselves. And most mistakes have no more significance than tripping over a kerbstone. Most of them turn out to be useful, too, as you can learn something from them, like to look where you are going more carefully.

Doing experiments such as the ones we've described here will help you to break the vicious cycles that otherwise keep the problem going. They will help you to do more of the things that you would like to do, and help you to feel more comfortable about doing them. They work by providing a new source of information. This helps you to think again about these mistakes, or ways in which you suppose that your behaviour might have been wrong.

Some general points about doing things differently

Keep going

When it comes to changing behaviour, some people give up because they do not think that they have made any progress. This can happen even though their friends and family can see a change.

Take care not to underrate your achievements. Watch out for upsetting thoughts about your progress. Progress may seem slow at first but it will gradually become more substantial and more noticeable to you. If it was easy, you would have done it before.

You might also find it much easier to remember the things that went badly than those that went well, or those that just felt normal. Perhaps the difficult times seem more important, as well as more distressing, than the easy ones, which then get forgotten.

Remember to keep a written record of what you are doing so that you can look back and check how far you've come. You're bound to be pleasantly surprised at the improvement over time.

Acknowledge your achievements

If you learn how to praise yourself for your successes, your confidence will grow faster. Each time you achieve something it is a success. Small successes turn into larger successes. Give yourself credit for all of them. Make a habit of giving yourself a mental pat on the back, and see if you can get someone else to notice your achievements. If you have a colleague, friend or relative who knows about your difficulties, maybe you could tell them, as well as writing it all down in this workbook.

Most people underrate their achievements to start with. This is particularly likely to happen if the risks you decide to take involve doing things that most people seem to find easy, like ordering a meal, or saying no when someone asks you to do something.

Here are some examples of how people downgrade their successes. Below each of these upsetting thoughts you will find an example of the sort of answer that might be more helpful.

Thought: *'Yes, but anyone could do that.'*
Answer: *'Not if they felt as anxious as you.'*

Thought: *'I should have done it better.'*
Answer: *'I will, in time. Now I will do what I can. No one could do more than that.'*

Thought: *'No one else would think that was important.'*
Answer: *'Maybe not. But I know how important it is to me.'*

It's worth remembering...

Downgrading your success makes you feel bad, and it makes it hard to keep trying.

Upsetting thoughts, as already mentioned, affect both your feelings and your behaviour. Make sure you know how to deal with them. Encouragement works far better than criticism because it makes you feel better and helps you to keep trying.

Encourage yourself as you would encourage anyone who was learning how to do something new. Try not to criticize or undermine yourself. If doing new things makes you more anxious, then remember that this kind of anxiety is likely to be temporary. The gains you make will last if you keep on doing them.

Dealing with setbacks

Everyone has 'ups and downs', and what you did successfully yesterday may seem impossible today. It is important to realize that setbacks are a normal part of progress and that you need not be discouraged by them.

- If at any stage you seem to be stuck, or even to have slid backwards, it could be because you are trying to run before you can walk. Recognize that you may have to take things slowly, and that breaking old patterns of thinking and of behaving takes time. Sometimes you will find the old ways of keeping yourself safe re-emerge, but what can change once can do so again. Even a small change means that you are not stuck with the problem, but need to keep working on it.

- Watch out for feeling discouraged, and use your new thinking skills to keep the setback in perspective. Everyone should expect a few setbacks, so when they happen to you try to take them in your stride, and do not let them interfere with your plans. If you do not give up you will overcome the problem in the end.

- Setbacks are often more apparent than real. You may have a bad day because you were tired or not very well. It is not that you have got worse, but rather that being tired or unwell makes everything you do a bit harder.

- Other people may unexpectedly plunge you into a situation that you were not yet ready for. For instance they might suggest that you come with them to a disco, or ask you to explain why you disagreed with a decision made at work. Remember that other people are far less aware of your anxiety than you are. They may not even notice it at all.

Try not to let a bad patch spread. If you need time to take stock, to muster your strength and your energy, then take that time before you continue making the changes that you find most difficult.

Adopting an 'ever ready' attitude

If keeping yourself safe keeps the problem going, then taking risks helps to overcome it. So take every opportunity that arises and, for instance, go to the pub or talk to someone in a bus queue if you have an unexpected chance to do so. You will find that you will improve faster and that ordinary everyday activities become less of a strain. You will no longer react to them as if they were really dangerous or frightening.

Try to stop keeping yourself safe even when doing everyday tasks. Instead of buying what you want without a word, deliberately talk to shop assistants or cashiers. Look at ordinary activities to see if you can find a way of turning them into useful ways of making progress.

Make a list here of some small, everyday things you could do to increase your level of interaction with other people.

What if taking risks, and doing things differently, makes me very anxious?

You will not be able to overcome the problem without experiencing some degree of anxiety, but the more confident you become the faster this will diminish. Think of handling your anxiety differently at different times: before, during or after taking the risk of doing something differently.

Beforehand

Once you have decided to go ahead and do something difficult it is sensible not to keep dwelling on it. It is not wise to give free rein to your imagination when thoughts or images of potential disasters come to mind. These will only make you feel worse. It is more helpful to stick with your decision to act, and then to distract yourself in any way you can to stop yourself worrying about it. Keep yourself as busy and occupied as possible. Re-read Section 2, page 33 for more ideas about how to do this.

After the event

Try to stop yourself going in for a 'post mortem'. Looking back at what happened from the point of view of someone with social phobia, it is only too easy to interpret everything that happened in terms of your own sense of failure, inadequacy or distress. Post mortems of this kind are as unlikely to be accurate as exaggerated 'fishy' stories about the size of the one that got away.

At the time

The key to coping with your feelings at the time is to pay less attention to them. Focus more on what is happening around you and less on your internal thoughts, feelings and self appraisals. Re-reading Section 2 may be helpful if you are finding this difficult.

Summary

1   Doing things differently is one of the most productive ways to build your confidence.

2   The way to do this is to think of yourself as carrying out small experiments, to find out what happens when you change your behaviour.

3   Experiments can help you give up using safety behaviours which otherwise keep the problems going.

4   Facing things instead of avoiding them also breaks one of the maintaining cycles, and experimenting with behaving this way makes it easier to do.

5   There are many ways in which experiments can help you to change your behaviour, and you might be able to think of more ways for yourself.

6   It is less important to worry about whether you will do things wrong, or break a social convention, than to start doing things in the way that you really would like to.

7   When thinking back on the things that you have done differently it is important not to dismiss or discount your successes. Doing new things may make you more anxious at first, but it will also help to build your confidence in the long run.

Well done! You have now completed Part Two. Part Three, the final part, explains how to build up your confidence and become more assertive, overcome underlying beliefs, deal with the legacy of being bullied and teaches some relaxation techniques that can help make social interactions easier.

Extra Charts and Worksheets

Alcohol use record

Date and event	Units of alcohol	How I felt at the time	How I felt the next day

Alcohol use record

Date and event	Units of alcohol	How I felt at the time	How I felt the next day

Alcohol use record

Date and event	Units of alcohol	How I felt at the time	How I felt the next day

Alcohol use record

Date and event	Units of alcohol	How I felt at the time	How I felt the next day

The two-way experiment worksheet

Step 1. Focus on yourself for three to five minutes.

(a) Notice everything that is going on inside you. For example, notice all the sensations that you can feel; how cold or hot you are; whether you are hungry, or tired, or full of aches and pains. Notice how your clothes feel on your body. Notice your feelings, and any thoughts, images, impressions or memories that come to mind.

(b) Answer the assessment questions (write your answers down):

1. How did you feel when focusing on yourself _____

2. What did you notice? Write down as much as you can here.

_____

_____

Step 2. Focus on things outside yourself for three to five minutes.

(a) Notice other people: how they look, what they are wearing, what they might be feeling or thinking about.

(b) Answer the two assessment questions (write your answers down):

1. How did you feel when focusing outside yourself _____

2. What did you notice? Write down as much as you can here.

_____

_____

Step 3. Compare the two.

What was different? _____

What was the same? _____

Step 4. Summarize your conclusions: **Self focus**   **Other focus**

Which made you feel better?

_____

Which gave you more of the information
that helps you along socially?

_____

Was focusing on other people difficult to achieve?
How did you do it?

_____

Do you need more practice to achieve the
desired effect?

The two-way experiment worksheet

Step 1. Focus on yourself for three to five minutes.

(a) Notice everything that is going on inside you. For example, notice all the sensations that you can feel; how cold or hot you are; whether you are hungry, or tired, or full of aches and pains. Notice how your clothes feel on your body. Notice your feelings, and any thoughts, images, impressions or memories that come to mind.

(b) Answer the assessment questions (write your answers down):

1. How did you feel when focusing on yourself_____

2. What did you notice? Write down as much as you can here.

_____

_____

Step 2. Focus on things outside yourself for three to five minutes.

(a) Notice other people: how they look, what they are wearing, what they might be feeling or thinking about.

(b) Answer the two assessment questions (write your answers down):

1. How did you feel when focusing outside yourself_____

2. What did you notice? Write down as much as you can here.

_____

_____

Step 3. Compare the two.

What was different?_____

What was the same?_____

Step 4. Summarize your conclusions: **Self focus**   **Other focus**

Which made you feel better?

_____

Which gave you more of the information
that helps you along socially?

_____

Was focusing on other people difficult to achieve?
How did you do it?

_____

Do you need more practice to achieve the
desired effect?

The two-way experiment worksheet

Step 1. Focus on yourself for three to five minutes.

(a) Notice everything that is going on inside you. For example, notice all the sensations that you can feel; how cold or hot you are; whether you are hungry, or tired, or full of aches and pains. Notice how your clothes feel on your body. Notice your feelings, and any thoughts, images, impressions or memories that come to mind.

(b) Answer the assessment questions (write your answers down):

1. How did you feel when focusing on yourself _____

2. What did you notice? Write down as much as you can here.

_____

_____

Step 2. Focus on things outside yourself for three to five minutes.

(a) Notice other people: how they look, what they are wearing, what they might be feeling or thinking about.

(b) Answer the two assessment questions (write your answers down):

1. How did you feel when focusing outside yourself _____

2. What did you notice? Write down as much as you can here.

_____

_____

Step 3. Compare the two.

What was different? _____

What was the same? _____

Step 4. Summarize your conclusions: **Self focus**   **Other focus**

Which made you feel better?

_____

Which gave you more of the information
that helps you along socially?

_____

Was focusing on other people difficult to achieve?
How did you do it?

_____

Do you need more practice to achieve the
desired effect?

The two-way experiment worksheet

Step 1. Focus on yourself for three to five minutes.

(a) Notice everything that is going on inside you. For example, notice all the sensations that you can feel; how cold or hot you are; whether you are hungry, or tired, or full of aches and pains. Notice how your clothes feel on your body. Notice your feelings, and any thoughts, images, impressions or memories that come to mind.

(b) Answer the assessment questions (write your answers down):

1. How did you feel when focusing on yourself_____

2. What did you notice? Write down as much as you can here.

_____

_____

Step 2. Focus on things outside yourself for three to five minutes.

(a) Notice other people: how they look, what they are wearing, what they might be feeling or thinking about.

(b) Answer the two assessment questions (write your answers down):

1. How did you feel when focusing outside yourself_____

2. What did you notice? Write down as much as you can here.

_____

_____

Step 3. Compare the two.

What was different?_____

What was the same?_____

Step 4. Summarize your conclusions: **Self focus**   **Other focus**

Which made you feel better?
_____

Which gave you more of the information
that helps you along socially?
_____

Was focusing on other people difficult to achieve?
How did you do it?
_____

Do you need more practice to achieve the
desired effect?

Thought record for identifying thoughts

Situation (be specific)	Feelings (there may be more than one)	Thoughts, impressions, etc. (keep the different thoughts separate)

Thought record for identifying thoughts

Situation (be specific)	Feelings (there may be more than one)	Thoughts, impressions, etc. (keep the different thoughts separate)

Thought record for identifying thoughts

Situation (be specific)	Feelings (there may be more than one)	Thoughts, impressions, etc. (keep the different thoughts separate)

Thought record for identifying thoughts

Situation (be specific)	Feelings (there may be more than one)	Thoughts, impressions, etc. (keep the different thoughts separate)

Thought record for looking for alternatives

Upsetting thoughts	Possible alternatives

Thought record for looking for alternatives

Upsetting thoughts	Possible alternatives

Thought record for looking for alternatives

Upsetting thoughts	Possible alternatives

Thought record for looking for alternatives

Upsetting thoughts	Possible alternatives

Complete thought record

Situation	Upsetting thoughts	Possible alternatives	Change in feelings (−10 to +10)	Action plan

Complete thought record

Situation	Upsetting thoughts	Possible alternatives	Change in feelings (−10 to +10)	Action plan

Complete thought record

Situation	Upsetting thoughts	Possible alternatives	Change in feelings (–10 to +10)	Action plan

Complete thought record

Situation	Upsetting thoughts	Possible alternatives	Change in feelings (−10 to +10)	Action plan

Thought record for changing behaviours

Specific situation (Think of a situation in which you use a safety behaviour)	Prediction (What will happen if you do not keep yourself safe? How will you know if it happens?)	Experiment (How will you find out? What will you do differently?)	What actually happened? (What did you observe? Stick to the facts.)	Conclusions (What does this mean?)

Thought record for changing behaviours

Specific situation (Think of a situation in which you use a safety behaviour)	Prediction (What will happen if you do not keep yourself safe? How will you know if it happens?)	Experiment (How will you find out? What will you do differently?)	What actually happened? (What did you observe? Stick to the facts.)	Conclusions (What does this mean?)

Thought record for changing behaviours

Specific situation (Think of a situation in which you use a safety behaviour)	Prediction (What will happen if you do not keep yourself safe? How will you know if it happens?)	Experiment (How will you find out? What will you do differently?)	What actually happened? (What did you observe? Stick to the facts.)	Conclusions (What does this mean?)

Thought record for changing behaviours

Specific situation (Think of a situation in which you use a safety behaviour)	Prediction (What will happen if you do not keep yourself safe? How will you know if it happens?)	Experiment (How will you find out? What will you do differently?)	What actually happened? (What did you observe? Stick to the facts.)	Conclusions (What does this mean?)

Thought record for facing fears

Specific situation (Think of a situation that you avoid)	Prediction (What will happen if you do not avoid this?)	Experiment (How will you face your fear? What will you do?)	What actually happened? (What did you observe? Stick to the facts)	Conclusions (What does this mean?)

Thought record for facing fears

Specific situation (Think of a situation that you avoid)	Prediction (What will happen if you do not avoid this?)	Experiment (How will you face your fear? What will you do?)	What actually happened? (What did you observe? Stick to the facts)	Conclusions (What does this mean?)

Thought record for facing fears

Specific situation (Think of a situation that you avoid)	Prediction (What will happen if you do not avoid this?)	Experiment (How will you face your fear? What will you do?)	What actually happened? (What did you observe? Stick to the facts)	Conclusions (What does this mean?)

Thought record for facing fears

Specific situation (Think of a situation that you avoid)	Prediction (What will happen if you do not avoid this?)	Experiment (How will you face your fear? What will you do?)	What actually happened? (What did you observe? Stick to the facts)	Conclusions (What does this mean?)

Thoughts and Reflections

Thoughts and Reflections

Thoughts and Reflections

Thoughts and Reflections

144

Thoughts and Reflections

Thoughts and Reflections

Thoughts and Reflections